# Vertically Integrated Architectures

## Versioned Data Models, Implicit Services, and Persistence-Aware Programming

Jos Jong

Apress®

*Vertically Integrated Architectures: Versioned Data Models, Implicit Services, and Persistence-Aware Programming*

Jos Jong
AMSTELVEEN, The Netherlands

ISBN-13 (pbk): 978-1-4842-4251-3          ISBN-13 (electronic): 978-1-4842-4252-0
https://doi.org/10.1007/978-1-4842-4252-0

Library of Congress Control Number: 2018966806

Managing Director, Apress Media LLC: Welmoed Spahr
Acquisitions Editor: Louise Corrigan
Development Editor: James Markham
Coordinating Editor: Nancy Chen

Cover designed by eStudioCalamar

Cover image designed by Freepik (www.freepik.com)

Distributed to the book trade worldwide by Springer Science+Business Media New York, 233 Spring Street, 6th Floor, New York, NY 10013. Phone 1-800-SPRINGER, fax (201) 348-4505, e-mail orders-ny@springer-sbm.com, or visit www.springeronline.com. Apress Media, LLC is a California LLC and the sole member (owner) is Springer Science+Business Media Finance Inc (SSBM Finance Inc). SSBM Finance Inc is a **Delaware** corporation.

For information on translations, please e-mail rights@apress.com, or visit www.apress.com/rights-permissions.

Apress titles may be purchased in bulk for academic, corporate, or promotional use. eBook versions and licenses are also available for most titles. For more information, reference our Print and eBook Bulk Sales web page at www.apress.com/bulk-sales.

Any source code or other supplementary material referenced by the author in this book is available to readers on GitHub via the book's product page, located at www.apress.com/9781484242513. For more detailed information, please visit www.apress.com/source-code.

Printed on acid-free paper

*I dedicate this book to the worldwide software engineering community.*

*Stay curious, keep innovating, and push our profession forward.*

# Table of Contents

# About the Author

 **Jos Jong** is a self-employed independent senior software engineer and software architect. He has been developing software for more than 35 years, in both technical and enterprise environments. His knowledge ranges from mainframes, C++, and Smalltalk to Python, Java, and Objective-C. He has worked with numerous different platforms and kept studying to learn about other programming languages and concepts. In addition to developing many generic components, some code generators, and advanced data synchronization solutions, he has prototyped several innovative database and programming language concepts. He is an abstract thinker who loves to study the fundamentals of software engineering and is always eager to reflect on new trends. You can find out more about Jos on his blog (`https://josjong.com/`) or connect with him on LinkedIn (`www.linkedin.com/in/jos-jong/`) and Twitter (@jos_jong_nl).

# Acknowledgments

There are many people who encouraged me to push forward with my ideas and eventually write this book. I'd like to thank all of them for inspiring me. Colleagues who were skeptical at the time helped me to rethink and refine certain aspects of my vision. I want to thank them for the interesting discussions. To the members of Know-IT, a group I have been a member of for ten years, my special thanks for all the patience you have shown me when I was suggesting better solutions again and again in whatever discussions we were having. I want to thank the people who read my early drafts: my good friends Marc, Rudolf, Edwin, Winfried, Peter-Paul, and especially Remco for doing most of the initial translations and essentially being the first full peer-reviewer. I also would like to thank Robbert, for all the inspirational words and for setting deadlines. And special thanks to my sister, Marian, my parents, my good friends Ger, Wilma, Nina, Sudais, and others who supported me.

# Preface

I guess most books start with lots of half-related notes and ideas. So far, so good. But my first notes and drawings date back 30 years. During my studies, I learned about *real* databases and how they magically hide a lot of technical details from the programmer.

With SQL, I saw the beauty of a fully thought through conceptual data model, brought to life by a neat and powerful query language. However, I also remember asking myself whether tables are really such a good choice to represent data. The relational model was obviously better than anything else out there. But influenced by other methods I studied, such as Sjir Nijssen's natural language information analysis method (NIAM), I imagined data more as a network of abstract objects (facts) joined together by relationships. In SQL, you have to specify the actual relationships, based on attributes, with every query, again and again. And because applications are mostly not built using SQL, every query also requires its own glue code, to fit inside the accompanying 3GL programming language. Why? These early thought experiments eventually became the main premise of this book.

Why doesn't the user interface understand the underlying data model, so that a lot of things can be arranged automatically? Why do we program in two, three, or four languages to build a single application? And why do we manually have to pass around strings with pieces of keys and data, as we do with JSON nowadays?

My inspiration to resolve these dilemmas over and over is born of frustration, experimentation, study, and lots of discussions within my peer group. I never was a computer scientist and, as practical as I like to be, loved working on concrete projects. But I used every slightly more generic challenge in any project to think and experiment with potential solutions. It always helped me to go beyond merely passing around records between screens, for example, with generic data reporting solutions, code generation, when useful, and fancy synchronization solutions. I also started studying scientific papers on related subjects. All this comes together in this book.

In an attempt to convince people that two-tier architectures and the ideas behind 4GL/RAD-languages deserve a second chance, I start with a thorough analysis of where we stand. Although I agree that most contemporary architectural principles were born out of necessity, I will explain how they eventually led to mostly disconnected tiers that we have to cobble together repeatedly. True, this gives us a lot of flexibility, but it forces us to write a lot of code that could be deduced from the system's data model. It also results in a lot of code duplication across layers and tiers. I believe that at least 70%–80% of what we write does not concern the business logic the application is about.

At the same time, I recognize the problems with 4GL and RAD that made them fail. And although it helps that platforms such as OutSystems and Mendix reintroduced the 4GL approach under the name *low-code*, I still see problems. Code generation cannot optimize for every real-life scenario, merging lots of existing techniques sounds compatible but is very constraining at the same time, and the versioning of external interfaces is still troublesome, as in the nineties.

What we must pursue are fundamental new concepts that are general-purpose and flexible at the same time, not just trying to mimic what we currently do manually. I would like to preach going back to the drawing board, getting rid of the anxiety to create a totally new programming language, build an actual compiler, and escape today's dogmas.

I'm convinced that the second half of my book introduces, or at least seeds, solutions to escape the current dilemmas. With a single unified conceptual data model, we can build what I call implicit services and a persistence-aware programming language to express only pure business logic. I show that what has made two-tier architectures inflexible and not-general purpose so far is the lack of support for data model versioning and a more conceptual approach to data modeling.

I hope my book will inspire experienced developers to explore these ideas. I believe that the challenges will be an interesting pursuit for computer science students. Software development is still in its infancy. I hope that my contribution will steer us away from the endless stream of frameworks that we see today. Trying to solve each individual problem with a separate framework mostly brought us more complexity and certainly did not increase developer productivity for the last decade or so.

Most of my ideas take the form of what-if proposals. That is not because I haven't experimented with some of them. For example, I built a prototype to explore the persistence aware programming language that I present. It impressed some people, but, for now, it is not a real product. But who knows what the future will bring.

# CHAPTER 1

# The Problem

*Problems are not stop signs, they are guidelines.*

—Robert H. Schuller

Like being in a swamp. That is how it must feel if you end up in a software development team, after switching from another profession. Just when you think you have a firm grasp of things, someone comes along with yet another new concept, principle, or framework. You just want to finish that one screen you're working on. But there are larger stakes. And, to be honest, after listening to all the arguments, you're on the verge of being convinced. Another framework gets added to the project.

The accumulation of frameworks year after year must pay off. You would expect things to have gotten super easy. And yet, every time a new team member is added, it becomes apparent that the team has created its own little universe. The new guy or gal has to absorb all the frameworks he or she is not familiar with and learn a whole new set of architectural principles.

I am not talking here about commonsense principles every self-respecting software engineer is expected to know. The problem lies in the never-ending avalanche of new ideas and experiments that manifest in the form of still more new architectural principles and frameworks.

© Jos Jong 2019
J. Jong, *Vertically Integrated Architectures*,
https://doi.org/10.1007/978-1-4842-4252-0_1

As well-intended as they may be, it is impossible to master them all. Every new person on the team has to be brought up to speed before being able to contribute. Even the developers present when the architecture or framework was introduced will have had lengthy discussions as to how, what, and why of the most recent implementation. It may have been looking very promising in PowerPoint, but reality can be tough. Once the hatchet is buried, two factions remain. One has poured so much energy in the defense of all the principles, it cannot let go. That faction will continue to preach that if you *apply them properly,* the gains are huge. The other faction is glad the discussion is over. It gets back to work, *to get things done,* partly exercising *architecture in name only.*

Maybe we shouldn't make such a fuss about this. The information and communications (ICT) industry is in its infancy. Although we have been developing software for several decades now, there is still so much room for improvement that we should actually praise people for trying new things. But this comes with pitfalls. Many initiatives could be categorized as old wine in new bottles. We don't need yet another implementation of an existing concept. We need better concepts that last longer than the typical three-to-five-year life expectancy of many frameworks and architectural principles. We need a more fundamental approach.

# Never-Ending Complexity

Developing software is a complex endeavor. While one would have expected it to have gotten easier over time, the exact opposite seems true. Back in the day, one could build a whole system using Turbo Pascal, C#, Java, and some SQL. But today, before you know it, you're once again Googling the latest features of HTML, to see which browser does or does not support them. Your CSS files are getting out of hand, so you start generating them with Sass. And while you were using Angular previously, you're thinking about switching to React. Your CV is growing and growing.

One of your team members has a lot of experience with Node.js. He makes sure to mention this every lunchtime. The idea emerges to build that one new service with Node.js instead of with Java: "That's one of the benefits of microservices: to choose the best-fitting implementation for each service." We read about how efficient Node.js can be in asynchronously accessing multiple external services. Naturally, some team members, after ten years of doing Java projects, are up for something new. They get excited!

The Java faction has not been resting on its laurels either. It left behind a past with J2EE, Entity Beans, JSP, Hibernate, JSF, and numerous other frameworks and concepts. But after first adopting several flavors of Spring, the itch starts again. Someone on your team suggests implementing certain logic using the Actor model. The proof of concept was successful. The developers' screens now show information about the Actor framework more and more often. Challenge accepted.

The polyglotting school of thought embraces the idea of mastering multiple programming languages. And, of course, it makes sense to take a look at another programming language every now and then. You can learn about different programming styles. And that generally makes you a better programmer. The question, however, arises: What to do in five or ten years, when systems built with multiple languages have to be maintained? Sure, if you're cynical, this can be viewed as a guarantee of job security, but it can really burden the customer with additional costs and frustrations.

It is already difficult to find an experienced programmer, let alone a full stack developer with knowledge of exactly the languages, concepts, and frameworks utilized in a particular project. Naturally, part of the increased complexity results from the fact that we expect more from the applications we build. User interfaces today are much more advanced than the character-based screens of yesteryear. We access data from multiple sources, and we may have to serve millions of concurrent users. Despite all this, most of the complexity we encounter can be attributed to an industry that's rapidly evolving.

Let's conclude that it is nobody's fault. We are all involved in a quest to simplify software development, and we certainly don't want to go back to the old days. But the smorgasbord of concepts and techniques fragments the industry. The Internet has enabled the exchange of knowledge but also led to an ocean of new ideas, both good and bad. Instead of getting simpler, building an application is getting more complex.

# Data Models Everywhere

One of the creeds of software engineering is DRY—don't repeat yourself. However, if you take a look at the source code of any randomly selected system, you will see repetition happening everywhere, within layers and across layers and tiers. A huge proportion of the code we write is essentially just retrieving, converting, and returning the exact same data items, albeit in different contexts and in a variety of formats. Why are we writing all that code?

At its core, virtually all software consists of storing, processing, and displaying information. The structure of that information can be described as entities, attributes, and relationships. Every item in such a model will be reflected in the software you develop—in the names and types of columns of a table; in the names of classes, getters, and setters in the data types that those receive and return; in the JSON structures that are exchanged with the client or other systems; and I could go on. In the UI client itself, the data model will probably be reflected in HTML elements, JavaScript structures, source code, and even partly in CSS styles. All this results in the definition of a given entity, attribute, or relationship being expressed in, let's say, five to ten places, if not more.

This means that for every entity, attribute, or relationship added to the system, we have to write multiple pieces of code in different layers, probably even in different programming languages. The actual amount may depend on the development environment at hand. However, it is and remains manual labor. Adding an attribute might not be such a big deal, but with adding entities and relationships, there is typically more complexity involved.

The fact that a data model manifests itself in so many ways also leads to the duplication of code taking care of validations and constraints. Users prefer to have immediate feedback from the user interface when data entered does not fit certain constraints. But to be sure to never store invalid data, you want the same check to be repeated in the service layer as well. And maybe you would even have the database check it again. Now imagine we develop multiple UI clients (web, mobile), and we end up with three to five places in which we do the exact same validations for which we write, and maintain, specific pieces of code.

It is fair to say that while we mastered the art of code reuse in most programming languages, there is still one aspect that leads to a lot of code repetition, and that is the data model itself.

# Growing Insecurity

With half the planet now sharing its personal and business information via online services, you would expect software security to be rock solid. Instead, the number of data breaches has been on the rise for years (1,579 reported cases and 178 million accounts exposed in 2017 in the United States alone).[1]

How can it be that an industry with so much money and prestige at stake make and accept so many blunders? Undeniably, one reason is the aforementioned ever-increasing complexity. No matter how easy it can be to avoid a particular security threat, risks lurk at every level. Any nontrivial

---

[1]Statista, "Annual number of data breaches and exposed records in the United States from 2005 to 2018 (in millions)," www.statista.com/statistics/273550/data-breaches-recorded-in-the-united-states-by-number-of-breaches-and-records-exposed/, 2018.

service is made up of several software components: load balancers, hypervisors, virtual machines, operating systems, containers, application servers, databases, frameworks, let alone its own code. It requires a lot of joint effort from knowledgeable people to keep secure every corner of such a software stack. A problem can arise from something as little as a bug in the application's source code. But a suboptimal configuration of any of the involved components or not updating certain parts of the software stack can also result in a huge security scandal.

Specific security risks exist in the realm of authentication and authorization. While there are numerous standard solutions for these mechanisms, many are still, at least partly, coded by hand, sometimes just to avoid dependence on a third party, but also because the integration with a standard solution may be more difficult to do. As a consequence, the average programmer is often involved in low-level security, to a point where it becomes notoriously unsafe.

Finally, there is the risk of URL vulnerabilities. A URL can reveal a lot about the structure of a system. It often happens that people modify a URL and gain access to data they are not authorized to. Once again, this problem exists because programmers have to identify and cater to these risks themselves.

There is obviously no excuse for being lazy about software security. But with the current state of ICT, it is as if we are trying to keep the general public out of private rooms in an office building that is a labyrinth of floors and little rooms with doors and windows everywhere, while we attempt to construct some of the key locks ourselves.

# Architectural Fog

Software architecture can be both the solution and the cause of problems. As mentioned, no matter how good the intentions of architects, they may cast a team into a fog-laden land, and fairly often, the benefits they promise are never realized.

Architecture is about having a blueprint, in the form of guidelines, for how to construct a system. Building software is a relatively new phenomenon. Especially because of the continuous influx of new ideas, it is good to agree on a number of principles. First is to achieve consistency, in the sense of avoiding every programmer doing things in his/her own way, but also to gain advantages, in terms of scalability, performance, and future proofing. Sadly, there are many ways in which this can get derailed.

The preferences of the particular architect play a part. If such a person is close to the software development process, is experienced, is able to maintain a good overview, and is able to translate this to a blueprint for the team, there is potential for a solid foundation. Not every architect, however, is that skilled, let alone capable of conveying a vision to the team. Plenty of things can go wrong in this regard.

I've already discussed the fact that we are bombarded by so many different architectural visions and that some architectures can fuel a lot of debate. Take the idea of microservices, for example. Everybody understands the wisdom of partitioning a bigger system into subsystems, either because there are multiple owners or stakeholders or simply because the whole is too large to be managed by a single team. But microservices take this idea one step further, resulting in an ongoing debate on how small, tiny, or microscopic a *micro*service should or must be.

Combining different architectural concepts can be another challenge. Ideas may work in isolation, but having them work together in a meaningful way might introduce some dilemmas. Or what if they don't fit a particular environment very well. Perhaps the concept is very useful for a certain industry but way too excessive for your current project.

One could see architecture as an unsolidified framework, especially in light of the fact that we have so much freedom with the current third-generation programming languages (3GL), this creates a need for blueprints. The more a language and its accompanying frameworks steer you in a particular direction, the less need there is for an *architectural story*.

The freedom to choose a different architecture for each project is cool and exiting. However, when it comes to quickly building robust and secure systems, it's rather sad that every team has to reinvent the wheel.

# Language Wars

Software exists by virtue of programming languages. So, you would expect them to improve every year, to help us out with all the issues mentioned so far in this chapter. The general perception is that they do. But do they? It is also commonly accepted that frameworks can be used to extend a programming language. But is that really true?

Virtually all software is built with 3GLs today. And these languages did indeed evolve. Object orientation, garbage collection, and exception handling became a standard feature for many languages. And such things as closures, coroutines, and functional extensions are getting more and more popular. However, object orientation was invented with Simula and Smalltalk in the sixties and seventies. The same is true for closures and functional programming. And coroutines have been at the core of Erlang since the eighties. So, what we mostly see is cherry-picking from other programming languages, both old and contemporary. In that sense, the *my-language-is-better-than-yours* approach is mostly about syntactic sugaring. There is nothing wrong with that. But what about our more fundamental needs?

While almost no software system can do without storing data and network communications, 3GLs are only concerned with in-memory data handling and processing. That's why we still deal with data persistency as a second-class citizen. The same is true for client-server communication. This is where code plumbing comes in. A lot of source code deals with the marshaling and unmarshaling of messages, filling and extracting screen data, or assembling and processing database queries. Recall that fourth-generation languages (4GL) in the nineties delivered in this area. There may be good reasons why we have stuck to 3GLs since then. It is still interesting, nonetheless, to see what we can learn from that era.

You may think that a smart 3GL-based framework can be as good as a language with integrated persistency and data communication. And, yes, frameworks can soften the sharp edges, in this respect, but they will never fundamentally solve all the related challenges.

Frameworks have been used forever, to simplify the interaction with the database or to invoke remote services. From Entity Beans to Hibernate, and from EJB to SOAP, all have been implemented using frameworks, either by using runtime reflection or code generation, each with their own range of problems and added complexity. Deeper integration to solve these issues can never be achieved, because one simply cannot augment a language at the level.

This is because frameworks play a particular role within a programming language. The language itself offers the programmer a host of abstractions and features that, in theory, allow the development of every conceivable construct. A framework, on the other hand, is basically just a collection of data structures and accompanying functions. This makes it impossible to add a truly new abstraction to a language by utilizing a framework.

Consider memory management. To add garbage collection to a language, one has to gain control over every creation of an object and, possibly, every reference to an object. In most languages (C++ could be regarded an exception here), this is utterly impossible to achieve.

Another example is the concept of coroutines. Think of coroutines as mini-processes, in that they are suspended when waiting for blocking I/O, while giving other coroutines the chance to continue their execution. The implementation of coroutines is typically based on the concept of segmented stacks, which can be enlarged on demand. How software deals with a stack is so intrinsically linked to the compiler and accompanying runtime that such an abstraction cannot really be implemented with a framework.

So, adding frameworks cannot compensate for a language lacking certain features. Some features just require a more fundamental and integrated approach.

This is certainly true for data persistency and data communication. As long as we keep trying to use frameworks to implement these aspects, we will never be able to write source code in terms of persistent or remote data. A programming language not being aware of what is really happening in this sense is like having a constant impedance mismatch between the intentions of the programmer and the programming language, with code plumbing and suboptimal execution as a result.

So, yes, languages did evolve. Take garbage collection. That has proven to be a great success. It prevents memory leaks and simplifies our code dramatically. We also see functional programming features that made their way to 3GL, for example, making it easier to write compact expressions to handle collections. But while being the main features of any application, persistency and network communication have remained the neglected stepchildren and are the main cause of large amounts of plumbing recurring in every software project.

# Frameworks by the Dozen

Frameworks can keep us from reinventing the wheel, but, as mentioned, the market is flooded with them. Their quality varies greatly, and because the framework du jour is replaced by something *better* the following year, we could be creating legacy code every day.

Now and then, this demands a responsible response to the following questions by every software developer and architect: Do I stay with the old? Do I use that hot new framework everybody is raving about? Or will I ever be a frontrunner, by pouring my heart and soul into something completely new?

One factor in this balancing act is the perceived quality of these pieces of art. It is a plus when a framework is widely used. This makes it stand up under scrutiny. But even then, the question remains whether it is maintained well enough, and how much priority is given to fixing bugs. It is a good thing for something to be open source, but it is still tough to tell your client that a given bug is caused by a framework, and you either have to dive into the dark secrets of that framework or wait for others to fix it.

Besides this, popularity and quality are not constant over time. Perhaps the initiators have already moved on to the next great idea. They take a few shortcuts, and along the way the quality of the product begins to suffer, all while there is a huge lock-in for your own project.

A framework may also constrain you. Not every framework plays well with other frameworks. That means the choice of a framework cannot be viewed independently of that of others. Sometimes frameworks overlap; sometimes they interfere; and sometimes they force you into using other frameworks.

As mentioned at the beginning of this chapter, frameworks may be intended to simplify things, but they can just as easily increase overall complexity. While it is nice to have these extensive lists on our résumés, if we're not careful, we are creating legacy code every single day. It requires a lot of experience and a pragmatic approach to not bog down a project in unnecessary complexity. The big question that we should ask ourselves is why do we need so many frameworks anyway?

# Summary

In this chapter, I have discussed the following:

- The ICT landscape is very immature and is, therefore, constantly on the move.

- Software development, in a way, is getting more complex rather than simpler.

- There is a lot of code repetition, owing to the data model having to be represented in different ways in multiple layers and tiers.

- Software security can partly be blamed by the complexity of the platforms we use and the low-level code we sometimes have to write with regard to authorization and authentication.

- Although the whole point of software architecture is to provide a steady foundation, new architectural ideas come along every year.

- 3GLs do not cater to two of the most essential aspects of any software system: data persistency and data communication. To use frameworks to compensate for that is a suboptimal solution.

- To help us out with some of these issues, we use a lot of frameworks. But that creates new problems and legacy every day.

After this pile-up of misery, some people may wonder why anyone would still want to become a programmer. But that's not how it works with professionals. Developing software is an inherently complex profession that requires a certain drive to get ahead. That we have to write more code than what would strictly be necessary is not the end of the world. And the fact that the complexity of the trade continues to increase is perhaps even a bonus for all those professionals who by their nature always want to learn new things and thrive on challenges.

However, something lurks beneath the surface. The vast amount of copycat code that we write again and again undoubtedly takes time. And time equals money. It makes projects take longer. More code also increases the risk of introducing bugs, which raises the demand for testing and leads to higher operational costs. More lines of code also make it harder to modify a system, because it implies more dependencies and a bigger impact by any change requested.

Besides all this, we cannot ignore the fact that it becomes more and more difficult to find good programmers. And things won't improve if we continue to increase the complexity of the profession, expecting candidates to have résumés with endless lists of acronyms. It is cool to be a full stack developer who knows all the tricks of the trade, but an ivory tower getting higher and higher is not going to benefit our clients in the long term.

The big question in this book is how to get out of this impasse. Therefore, in Chapter 3, I will provide a complete analysis of all the problems mentioned so far. But because we can certainly learn from mistakes made in the past, I will first delve into a bit of history in Chapter 2.

# CHAPTER 2

# History: How Did We Get Here?

*A people without the knowledge of their past history, origin and culture is like a tree without roots.*

—Marcus Garvey

The landscape of programming languages, concepts, and frameworks that we see today did not appear out of thin air. And there is plenty to learn from this past. Therefore, before I start talking about solutions, in the next chapters, it is of value to study why we do things the way we do. It will help us to broaden our view and give us the opportunity to learn from both historic failures and successes.

In the nineties, when fourth-generation languages (4GL) and Rapid Application Development (RAD) tools gained popularity, to add a new attribute to an application, you could just change the database schema and adapt the related screen definitions. There was no such thing as a service layer to be rewritten or deployed. And with the introduction of object databases later on, there finally seemed to be a solution for the impedance mismatch between object-oriented programming languages and databases. There are so many concepts we can still draw inspiration from, if only by understanding why these concepts exited stage left.

© Jos Jong 2019
J. Jong, *Vertically Integrated Architectures*,
https://doi.org/10.1007/978-1-4842-4252-0_2

Some may just have been ahead of their time. Others were limited in functionality, getting too complex in certain scenarios, lacking compatibility and openness, or just becoming less popular, owing to changing market situations.

It is no different with all the hundreds of frameworks that are added to GitHub every year. Of course, all these initiatives are praiseworthy, but even frameworks end up in the garbage can more often than not. Some may be built on a great idea but were badly implemented, lacking sufficient functionality, or did not appear as simple as the `README.md` seemed to suggest.

We must realize that sometimes true progress cannot be made unless we take a few steps back. Back to the drawing board, as they say. Innovation is not fueled by simply stacking upon existing techniques. Once in a while, we must return to the roots of earlier developments and take another direction.

# How and Why JSON Conquered

System integration with what we now call *services* is not a recent invention. As far back as the seventies, solutions were available in various flavors of remote procedure calls (RPCs). Later attempts to further abstract and standardize such remote interfaces, such as CORBA, EJB, and SOAP, in the end, gave way to plain and simple XML or JSON over HTTP. Let's dig into the hows and whys of these attempts and see what we can learn.

Connecting two software systems boils down to the exchange of data, in the sense of a message sent back and forth. If that happens in a synchronous way, we can view it as an RPC. In the seventies and eighties, there were numerous standards in vogue that operated on this principle, usually in the form of plain function calls, without an abstract concept such as a *component*, as was later introduced with CORBA.

They were mostly built around libraries, to take care of the marshaling and unmarshaling of messages into binary formats. But these standards were very much lacking compatibility with each other, because they were often associated with a particular programming language or application development environment. This didn't fly in an IT landscape that became increasingly heterogeneous. They were also relatively low level, with little or no support for higher-level abstractions, objects, or security.

In a response to this, solutions emerged that bridged the gap between both different operating systems (OSs) and programming environments, while at the same time, striving for a higher level of abstraction. Instead of simply invoking a remote procedure, one could now think in terms of objects or components. This was the realm of CORBA, EJB, and OLE—all of which appeared very promising at the time. Some were even designed in such a way that it did not matter whether a function was invoked locally or remotely, apart from the huge difference in performance, obviously.

But, as we know, this is not the end of the story. Many developers floundered when faced with the complexity of these standards. CORBA especially became notorious for its many concepts and accompanying acronyms—seemingly, way too much for something that essentially comes down to sending messages back and forth. EJB and OLE had the additional drawback of still being bound to a specific programming environment (Java and .NET, respectively).

One of the more fundamental problems was that there was no easy way to deal with multiple versions of components and functions—a serious issue in a world where the essence of having separate systems is that they can, or sometimes must, have their own release schedule. It was also difficult to stay away from a lot of complexity, such as generating stubs and skeletons or different ways of handling transactions. All this, while simplifying system-to-system communication was the core goal of these developments.

It is worth mentioning the introduction of *entity beans* as part of the Java J2EE standard. This was an attempt at go beyond remote components. It tried to deal with a remote system as a kind of remote-object database, but it was destined for failure. The implementation didn't take into account the impact of latency when querying individual objects, apart from the overhead resulting from the fact that every object was managed by its own network connection. The idea itself was sound, but as will become clear later in this book, something like this is only viable if you integrate it into the programming language, not as an afterthought.

Because of all this complexity, more and more developers leaned toward simply exchanging XML over HTTP. The term *web service* was born. Although this could be regarded as a step back in the level of abstraction, there were key advantages to the simplicity of this approach. Its shortcomings, like no standard for the serialization of certain data types, and no explicit support for transactions, sessions, and security, eventually led to the development of SOAP. SOAP stands for *Simple Object Access Protocol*. But *simple* was a deceptive term, because if you could say anything about SOAP, you would probably not say that it is simple.

Although SOAP is still used, many developers eventually started to send their own message formats over HTTP. And although AJAX (Asynchronous JavaScript and XML) for web browser development began with the idea of using XML, JavaScript Object Notation (JSON) was a better fit for a client that is written in JavaScript anyway. That's why JSON is now dominating the exchange of data between clients, servers, and external systems. All this is pretty much done *by example*. Nobody cares about schemas or a standard serialization for something such as a date value. The only idea that had any impact later was REST, which brought a little more structure to the use of HTTP methods and URLs.

So, we can say that after all these attempts to abstract the communication between system components by bringing them closer to the programming language, we are almost back to square one. The only difference with proprietary binary messages over TCP/IP is that we have now agreed to serialize data in the JSON format. This, together with a now commonly applied encoding, such as UTF-8, has become the de facto standard for system integration. And that's it.

What can we learn from this historic overview? We can conclude that simplicity trumps everything. The hot spot for the adoption of a concept is precisely where everyone immediately *gets it*. Abstractions and language integration would be great to ease the communication between systems, but not if the resulting implementation is many times more complex than something as simple as JSON. In other words, you can only beat JSON with something even simpler than JSON.

# How and Why We (Used to) Love Tables

Databases have a long and tumultuous history as well. Before the concept of a database was introduced, all exchange between programs was done using individual files. Databases have dramatically simplified data storage and retrieval, yet we still seem to be on a quest for the perfect solution, as is evident from the recent NoSQL trend.

The introduction in the sixties and seventies of hierarchical and network databases was a breakthrough innovation. After the introduction of random access persistent storage, it suddenly became possible to run random queries on all available data. This, however, required data to be stored in a specific, coherent, and transactional way. We needed a piece of software to govern this. With that, the database was born.

Hierarchical databases emphasized the hierarchical aspect of data. One-to-many relationships were modeled as tree-like structures. Not a bad idea in itself, but it had its limitations. In principle, access was only possible by means of the root nodes. It was difficult to define many-to-many relationships, and in many cases, to change the structure of the database, you had to make a completely new copy of it.

In that sense, the concept of a network database was an improvement, as relationships between record types could now be many-to-many, if required. While the hierarchical model had to rely on data redundancy or foreign keys to cope with many-to-many relationships, we were now able to completely normalize the data model. Every entity type could have its own record type. Still, even the network model was quite rigid.

The relational model[1] eventually brought the desired flexibility. Finally, there was a single conceptual model with a mathematical foundation that could support all operations and queries imaginable. It took a while before computing power was sufficient to give us a feasible implementation, but sometime in the nineties, the battle was over. If you needed a database, you picked a relational one.

Unfortunately, the relational theory and SQL proved not to be the holy grail. Relational database management systems (RDBMSs) were developed with administrative corporate environments in mind, not Internet applications with millions of concurrent users. New insights, such as the CAP theorem[2] and MapReduce,[3] inspired new designs that no longer emphasized the transactional consistency of the database but instead favored unlimited scalability. And although this new vision did not dictate what query language to use, SQL fell to the wayside as well.

The reason is probably mainly cultural. While SQL, with its plain-English syntax appears simple, in practice, its use is quite an ordeal for some developers, especially if the query becomes slightly more complex than two tables and a WHERE clause. Perhaps training related to this aspect

---

[1]E. F. Codd, "A Relational Model of Data for Large Shared Data Banks," *Communications of the ACM*, Vol. 13 (6), 1970, pp. 377–387.

[2]Eric Brewer, "Towards Robust Distributed System," *Proceedings of the Nineteenth Annual ACM Symposium on Principles of Distributed Computing*, July 16–19, 2000.

[3]Jeffrey Dean and Sanjay Ghemawat, "MapReduce: Simplified data processing on large clusters," *Proceedings of the 6th Symposium on Operating Systems Design and Implementation*, December 6–8, 2004.

was lacking, but it is likely also owing to the fact that in SQL, you have to specify what keys constitute a relationship in every query. If you combine that with some additional WHERE conditions to filter data, suddenly it is not that easy to validate the correctness of a query. And it doesn't get easier when you throw in such features as GROUP BY, HAVING, and EXISTS into the equation. This is why, despite SQL's power, many programmers have a love-hate relationship with it, no matter how sound its mathematical foundation.

It's great that in a NoSQL document-oriented database you can retrieve an entire JSON document in one go. In SQL, this could take multiple queries, simply because the result of a relational query, by definition, is a flat table with no possibility of representing hierarchical structures.

Yet, NoSQL is not the answer for everything. It might be simpler to store every user, blog post, or other main entity as a JSON document. But that's a very simplified view of the world (ignoring other types of NoSQL here for now). Perhaps you want to analyze data that involves multiple documents. In SQL, you simply join them together. In NoSQL, you would sometimes have to execute multiple queries for that. And although more and more NoSQL implementations support some way of joining data, it is still kind of an afterthought.

Way before NoSQL, in the nineties, when object-oriented languages gained popularity, multiple attempts were made to access a database in terms of objects. By having a database that follows the same structure as the programming language, you effectively removed the so-called impedance mismatch. After creating an object and assigning values to its properties, a save or commit operation would persist the object concerned into the database. Retrieval of data is done by means of initial queries (filters) but mostly by navigating from object to object. Relationships between objects are nothing more than pointers or lists of pointers. In this sense, it resembles the network database model, with a key difference being the direct mapping to the object-oriented programming language.

Although object-oriented database management systems (OODBMSs) such as Versant, now the Actian NoSQL Object Database (`www.actian.com/data-management/nosql-object-database/`), and Objectivity (`www.objectivity.com/`) are still used in certain niche environments, we hear very little about them anymore. The tight integration with a given programming language typically made these products dependent on that same language. That is far from ideal in a heterogeneous software environment. In addition, at the time, there were a lot of players in this market, all offering their own proprietary solutions. None of them ever grew toward a de facto standard. Even an attempt for official standardization by the Object Data Management Group (ODMG)[4] did not pay off.

However, a more fundamental problem of object databases occurred in a different area. Querying data in an object database is mostly done by navigating from object to object. All those individual inquiries can lead to a massive stream of synchronous I/O requests that limit the performance of the system. This is in contrast with SQL databases, which execute queries based on a query plan to optimize disk I/O as much as possible. With SQL, the programmer controls which specific queries get executed, making him/her able to know about and manually restrict the number of round-trips to the database server. Object databases, by their nature, must figure this out themselves, but they will never be able to predict upcoming data requests—at least not when data persistency has to be squeezed into an existing programming language.

Incidentally, the same network round-trip problem also plagued Java entity beans. Every programmer who dealt with an object-relational mapper (ORM), such as Hibernate, has had trouble with the negative effects of so-called lazy loading, which has a similar root cause.

---

[4]R.G. Cattell et al., eds., *The Object Data Management Standard: ODMG 3.0*, Morgan Kaufmann Series in Data Management Systems (Burlington, MA: Morgan Kaufmann, 2000).

What can we learn from this history and the current state of the art with regard to databases? It is obvious that we have been reaping benefits from the relational model. It has proven to be extremely powerful, and it is supported in every conceivable form throughout the IT landscape. But it has its share of problems. NoSQL helped to solve the problem with scaling but compromised this with less uniform structures that make certain types of queries more difficult. At the same time, the frequent use of object-relational mappers indicates that programmers do appreciate a tighter integration of data persistency within the programming language. An object database does exactly that but has a fundamental problem that it shares with object-relational mappers: unwanted lazy loading, with the risk of too many network round-trips. This is a challenging but interesting subject that I will refer to many times in the upcoming chapters, eventually working toward a solution.

# How and Why We Reverted to 3GL

Programming languages went through an interesting development. After the first assemblers, which retroactively were labeled second-generation languages (2GLs), we progressed from 3GL to 4GL, and there was even speculation about fifth-generation programming languages, each generation standing for a higher level of abstraction. But nobody talks about 4GL or 5GL anymore. Instead, all bets are on small variations of 3GLs such as Java, Python, Haskell, etc., and 3GL-based frameworks. Why did we step back? Let's see what happened.

After a period of programmers writing pure machine code, assemblers in the fifties provided the first major abstraction in programming languages: the abstraction of memory addresses. For the first time, it was possible to move around statements and data, letting the assembler compute the resulting memory layout in the sense of address offsets.

With the introduction of 3GLs, a number of large strides were made. It became possible to use operators to express the most common mathematical and logical operations in readable form. But more important was the introduction of functions. That was a major shift from assemblers, for which you had to manage everything around parameter passing and local variables by hand. Both of these function-related concepts are typically implemented using the call stack. So, we could say that the main thing 3GLs contributed was the abstraction of the stack. The management of memory other than the stack, typically called the heap, was generally still left for the programmer to handle manually.

Manual memory management, especially releasing memory at the right time, has long been a stumbling block in a lot of 3GLs. Languages such as LISP and Smalltalk already provided a solution for this, in the guise of garbage collection, but popular languages, such as Pascal, C, and C++, never provided a satisfactory solution for this. With the risk of memory leaks and unintentionally referencing released memory, both still cause trouble in so many applications.

In addition to internal memory, there is another type of memory that you can hardly avoid as a software developer: external memory. In traditional mainframe and minicomputer environments, for example, COBOL, there was a degree of support for accessing files and databases from within the language. But that was mainly based on the fact that the physical layout of records in internal memory was identical to that on disk. The introduction of SQL broke (justly so) with this kind of *tight integration*. The drawback, however, was that it introduced a separation between two worlds: one language, in which you express business logic, and another language, in which you write queries. This was the first manifestation of what later became known as the *impedance mismatch*.

Languages such as COBOL and C featured the phenomenon of *embedded SQL*, usually implemented by means of a pre-compiler. But APIs for database communication tended toward a model in which they accept

SQL in the form of pieces of text that get sent to the database with a generic API. This also made the handling of returned data a manual thing. Any form of integration was lost now. Later attempts to simplify this process again, with object-relational mappers, as previously mentioned, had varying degrees of success.

In the nineties, the industry was not yet resigned to a strict separation between programming language and database access. Database vendors developed their own programming languages that had complete, or at least better than 3GL, integration with the database. Take PL/SQL, for example, which allows direct access to the database.

A whole new industry flourished—that of 4GL languages, rapid application development (RAD), and computer-aided software engineering (CASE) tools. All had the same objective of tighter integration between the programming language, the underlying database, and the user interface. Sometimes, as with Oracle, interlinked with the accompanying database product, but in other cases, with plug-ins for every conceivable database engine or external interface. Screens and reports were typically defined in terms of database queries. This greatly contrasted with 3GLs, in which the gathering of data and filling a screen or building a report had to be coded from scratch.

For the development of administrative systems, these 4GL tools were a blessing. By speeding up development, you could save costs, take less time to implement new features, and make fewer mistakes. But if this was all true, why is no one talking about 4GL anymore? There are a number of reasons for this.

First, all of these products were very much proprietary developments. So, it was almost inevitable to be confronted with a major vendor lock-in, and the market quickly became fragmented, which made it hard to find developers with the required skills. There were lots of initiatives, and no one dared to predict which would survive in the long term.

But there were other factors involved. Some 4GLs were designed to have a sentence-like structure, such as with COBOL and SQL. This was probably thought of as being the result of a higher abstraction level. However, the more universal structure of 3GLs with objects and functions proved to be way more modular.

Yet another problem was that not all 4GL development environments were as extensible and open as one might have hoped. Businesses saw their software landscape become increasingly heterogeneous and complex, and the term *open systems* was the buzzword of that period. This was not a healthy substrate for proprietary 4GL applications.

The final blow came from the rise of the Internet and accompanying technologies. Rather than distributing software onto every PC, software developers started using the Internet browser as a kind of *smart terminal*. Graphical user interfaces (GUIs) were now built in HTML. Vendors of 4GL and RAD tool sets struggled. They released haphazard extensions to support HTML, but to no avail. A user interface in HTML, especially if you want full control over the screen layout, cannot simply be linked to a couple of database queries. And with the demand to also interact with arbitrary databases or external systems using such technologies as CORBA and SOAP, 4GL suddenly became a burden rather than a blessing. The advantages evaporated, and a lot of 4GL vendors became defunct.

A catalyst in this development was the emergence of Java. While initially developed for set-top boxes, Java proved the 3GL everyone has been waiting for. C++ was too unforgiving; COBOL started to show its age; and Smalltalk was quite CPU-intensive at the time. With Java, a general-purpose programming language appeared that had a familiar syntax and a garbage collector under the hood. Sun Microsystems eventually licensed Java under the GNU General Public License, and owing to the virtual machine (VM), the need to port software for different machine architectures became a thing of the past. All that was exactly what was needed for Internet-based application development.

Microsoft eventually accomplished the same with C#. And the 3GL landscape grew bigger by the day. Nobody talks about 4GL, let alone 5GL, anymore. But as you will see later in this book, we can learn from both the accomplishments and mistakes of that era.

Other than a few niche businesses, the industry en masse chose to go for 3GL-based development environments. We program in 3GLs that, other than the additions of object orientation and garbage collection, barely evolved in the last 50 years (I will refer to functional programming later in this book). Everything that is lacking from the language, we add using frameworks: a framework for accessing the database, a framework for the rendering of web pages, one for handling service requests, and even one for writing log files.

Of course, 3GLs are getting more and more powerful, with such features as pattern matching, implied typing, closures, and coroutines. But all of these concepts have existed since the seventies and eighties. They only became more mainstream owing to languages cherry-picking from one another. Regardless, these features all stay very close to the main 3GL abstractions: the handling of functions and the management of internal memory. They never solved fundamental challenges such as the support for data persistency, network communication, or user interaction.

The step back from 4GL to 3GL is very interesting, if we speculate about the future of programming. One after the other, clever 3GL frameworks prove how eager we actually are to simplify such things as accessing a database, the construction of services, or building user interfaces. Yet, the amount of plumbing in an average information system is still huge. We are on a quest for the right level of abstraction, but we certainly haven't found it yet.

# Summary

From this historic perspective, it appears we have plenty of reasons why we do things the way we do. However, it also shows an industry tripping over a number of promising developments and then taking a few steps back.

We went from 3GL to 4GL and back to 3GL again. In theory sound concepts such as CORBA and EJB were eventually superseded by low-level solutions based on HTTP and JSON. Object databases, in the end, proved not to be a viable alternative to relational databases, and NoSQL left many gains from relational databases by the wayside.

To compensate for all that, we collectively keep adding frameworks to our code bases. Every year, new frameworks step into the limelight, by garnering attention via conferences, web sites, and books, for all those who want to *stay ahead*. Résumés keep getting longer, and a lot of code we write is doomed to be labeled *legacy* in a few years. It would be interesting to see how sustainable this pattern is.

Maybe we need to step back more often. Returning to the drawing board, we can survey the lay of the land and ponder what it is we really require to leap forward, especially because we, as software developers, know that, in theory, everything is possible. Remember: it is all a matter of *make believe*.

# CHAPTER 3

# Analysis: What's Going Wrong?

*A programming language is low level when its programs require attention to the irrelevant.*

—Alan Perlis

The core question of this book is how to increase productivity and quality in software development. In Chapter 1, I discussed in particular how productivity has been stagnating for a while. I also surveyed past concepts and frameworks. Now it's time for more in-depth analysis: what's going wrong, and why.

Those who argue that nothing's wrong may have plenty of ammunition. Suppose we are building a web client. We build a neat service layer and put a database below that—a typical mainstream architecture. The principles that form the foundation for this best practice have their merits. In addition, the frameworks we use get better every day. So, we should expect our productivity and quality to grow, right? But will they? Smart tools keep our productivity going, but, as noted previously, frameworks can sometimes introduce more complexity than they solve.

We seem to have ended up in a paradox. Smarter frameworks and concepts ought to increase productivity and quality, but many of these clever solutions prove not to be as useful as they seem. While they solve problems in one area, they introduce new ones in others, which we then

© Jos Jong 2019
J. Jong, *Vertically Integrated Architectures*,
https://doi.org/10.1007/978-1-4842-4252-0_3

solve with even other smart solutions. This keeps us stumbling from concept to concept, in a world in which a stream of promising ideas never seems to dry up. So, the question remains: Are we actually moving forward?

As discussed before, a lot of the code we write can be deduced from the underlying conceptual data model. Having to write it manually takes time and money, increases the risk for bugs, and makes maintenance more expensive. Is it the architecture itself that gets in the way? That's something I will investigate, starting with this chapter.

You'll see the reasons why we see a multitude of repeating patterns in our code, and we learn how, fundamentally, frameworks cannot prevent this from happening. In addition to this, I will demonstrate why application developers still have to deal frequently with low-level issues. Being responsible for encoding, serialization, and escaping of data and text is a source of bugs that can lead to serious security vulnerabilities.

Also, taking a step back, I will look at the industry as a whole. I address a number of market factors and physiological factors that put the brakes on innovation.

# To DRY or Not to DRY

It is a mortal sin for every programmer: needless repetition of code. We even invented an acronym to combat it: DRY (don't repeat yourself). Functions exist to prevent repetition. They are also key in breaking up a problem into parts, simplifying the maintenance of code, and allowing us to share it with other developers in a structured fashion.

In combination with object-oriented concepts such as classes, we can even define whole frameworks. This, in theory, sounds like the way to eliminate all imaginable and unnecessary redundancy in source code. But take one look at the source code of your average information system, and you will observe repetition of structures and logic all over the place.

One type of repetition we see a lot is owing to transformations of one representation into another. In a serious system, let's say with hundreds of SQL tables, you can observe thousands of little pieces of code that transform the value from the column into one that fits in a Java, C#, or other in-memory object. In other parts of the system, you might see as much code transforming objects and attribute values to JSON or something similar. And in a web client, we might see another stockpile of code to transform values to HTML elements and vice versa.

If only this were limited to attributes containing strings and numbers, but entities are related to one another. And these relationships have a different representation at every level, as well, from taking the form of a foreign key in an SQL table to an in-memory array, then as a JSON array to, perhaps, finally, a JavaScript array or HTML DOM tree.

A large part of this code directly reflects the structure of the underlying persistent data model. So, the question is, why, despite all the possibilities of functions and classes, do we have to write all this code by hand?

The principal reason can be found in the programming languages we use. A 3GL, such as Java, PHP, or C#, has no notion of the conceptual data model that is behind the design of the system. It only knows how to deal with the structures we explicitly define with it. That is because 3GLs are only concerned with the management and manipulation of in-memory data. By definition, this means that we, as programmers, will always be concerned about how data exchange, with a database or over a network, is to be mapped onto those memory structures.

A framework, no matter how clever, will never be able to escape this limitation of a 3GL. You can get quite far with functions or classes helping you with some auxiliaries, such as conversions, checks, etc., but the actual mapping between the data that comes in and passes through virtually always must be specified explicitly.

It may be possible to define these mappings by way of a configuration file. Think of object-relational mapping (ORM), by which you hook up a database schema to an object model. But such solutions have their own share of problems. For example, however smart an ORM framework, it will never be able to predict what data in which order will be accessed from your source code. That can result in a large number of unnecessary round-trips to the database for relatively small queries. This is known as the "lazy-loading" problem. A 3GL framework can never solve this automatically, as it has no knowledge of the source code of the program under execution. Additionally, a 3GL's structure is conceptually very close to the underlying machine architecture, in the sense of a central processor with internal memory. It knows of no abstractions that can be employed to embody and analyze database access.

That many developers see the potential for transparent and automatic access to a database or external systems is not only evident from the existence of ORM tools but also, in the past, from the development of object databases, J2EE entity beans, CORBA, and Enterprise JavaBeans (EJB), to name a few. All of these had their own problems, and many were just too complex in practice.

Dynamic languages are able to avoid some of the 3GL limitations mentioned. Because they allow for a larger degree of reflection, you are able to virtualize or interpret things in runtime that are hard or impossible to realize in static programming languages. Think of the automatic mapping of URLs to function parameters, or how Ruby on Rails gained fame with the automatic mapping of properties and function calls to database structures and queries. But in a way, all these things remain workarounds.

A more radical solution is model-driven development (MDD). With MDD, a code generator takes care of all the plumbing. But often, you might want to combine generated code with bits of your own. The hope, thus, is that the underlying framework doesn't make this kind of interfacing needlessly complex. In addition, code generation is, more or less, creating a poor man's compiler. Generating code often results in increasingly long build times that can undo the pursued gain in productivity.

# Serving Business Logic

One argument that can be made against the reasoning in the last section is that not all data structures in a service implementation or client are a direct reflection of the underlying persistent data model. In addition to the one-to-one storage of data being entered, most information systems exist for the purpose of subsequently filtering and processing that data. Under such scenarios, we cannot do without manually written service implementations. Or can we?

Let's start with an example. Suppose you create a screen that, for a given customer, can show the top-ten products this customer ordered. This filtering of products is a clear example of business logic that is not a basic read/write operation. We could argue that the related service implementation, therefore, does not adhere to the pattern of repetition illustrated in the previous section. It is not just passing along data; it also combines, sorts, and filters data. However, if we zoom in on such a business-logic-specific service, we see something entirely different.

It is true that we will have to write specific code to determine the top-ten products a customer purchased. This may take the shape of a number of SQL joins with an ORDER BY and LIMIT clause. Or, alternatively, we might filter the data in memory. Regardless, the result of this filter is a collection of products. And while we could just return the ten product IDs (keys), we would often want to return a number of additional attributes concerning the products, to avoid the need for subsequent calls from the client to get the details of those products. Extra calls would mean more round-trips over the network, resulting in decreased responsiveness of the user interface.

Because of this, in the real world, we always have to trade off between two extremes: fine-grained services that can be combined like LEGO bricks vs. course-grained services that return as much data as possible for optimal performance. Returning more data in a single call, however, does not mean the structure of the returning data is less related to the underlying model. While the preceding product filtering example itself can be seen as specific business logic, the data returned is still in line with the underlying database. In other words, the result of a lot of data processing can still be expressed in terms of entities from the system's conceptual data model. The source code that performs the filtering may be specific, but in large parts of the source code of the service, we will still see the repetition of patterns, as described in the previous section.

In addition, every service method we add may lead to yet more repetition. Suppose we add some other services that filter products. While each of those services probably has its own unique bit of filter logic, a large part of the source code will be identical to that of the other services. We can try to solve this with the reuse of code, but owing to dependencies between the query language and the source code, this is not always as easy as it sounds, particularly when each of the services needs to return a different subset of attributes or related entities.

Besides filtering and reordering, services may also derive data in other ways. Suppose that in the preceding example, in addition to the top-ten products, we also want to know the percentage of sales represented by those ten products against all sales to the given customer. If we implement a separate service for this, it can be reused in conjunction with any other service. But as stated before, such a fine-grained service design is not wise, for performance reasons.

The results of mathematical operations may be viewed as derived, calculated, or virtual read-only attributes. We can also have virtual entities. For example, say a service returns the percentage of total sales by product per customer. The records returned by such a service have no representation within the conceptual data model (assuming we only model the state of the system, not derived data). It just refers to other entities, probably with a product key and a customer key. For that reason, we could see it as a derived or virtual entity, as with the result of a GROUP BY in SQL. The core of the service implementing this group-by logic cannot be derived from the conceptual data model, but as soon as we let the service return some related data (to prevent unnecessary round-trips), we are in the area of deducible logic again.

With this, we have covered three types of data processing: filtering, calculation, and grouping. Each of those relates to a specific type of element in data modeling.

- A filter may be viewed as a derived (virtual) relationship, in the preceding example, as a specific read-only one-to-many relationship between customers and products.

- A calculation (including string manipulation, and others) can be seen as a derived attribute.

- A group-by can be seen as a derived entity.

A service layer of a typical information system can involve a lot of these data transformations. That convinces many people that the complete data model externally exposed by a service API cannot be derived from the underlying database. They feel that a service layer creates a kind of different world than suggested by the underlying data model. But that— and that is the main point here—is not true.

The first reason is that all the operations mentioned nearly always exist alongside standard CRUD services, just because we must add and modify data. It is also rare that we subsequently only want to query purely derived data, if only to verify that the data entered is stored correctly. And let's not forget that an information system's purpose, besides processing data, is also to register and share data as it is.

I've already mentioned the second reason. For better performance, it is preferable that services that derive data also return related entities. So, the core of a service may be concerned with unique business logic (such as a filter, calculation, or group-by), but the rest will still be a one-to-one reflection of certain parts of the underlying data model.

In the end, it is all about the definition of the term *business logic*. If we define it as broadly as possible, every bit of data handling in a service layer could be considered business logic. If, however, we reserve the term *business logic* for specific logic that goes beyond basic data operations, we arrive at an interesting insight.

All CRUD actions can be directly derived from a data model. The same goes for the parts of service implementations that just return related data. Only the specific logic that pertains to filtering, calculation, or group-by escapes this criterion. With this viewpoint, only that logic is actual business logic.

If we look at an average information system using this definition, it may be only 10% to 30% of the source code in a service layer that can be considered pure business logic. The majority of the code can be qualified as repetition, as referred to in the previous section. We're wasting time writing code the system could have dreamt up itself.

# Tiers That Divide Us

You started this chapter learning that a lot of the code we write can be derived from the underlying data model. You have also learned that frameworks cannot help us out in this respect, because they cannot escape the fact that 3GLs have no notion of the conceptual data model that is behind the design of the system.

All this was discussed with a service layer in mind. But the problem is larger than that. A modern software architecture consists of multiple layers and tiers, and within every layer, the data model reappears. While it is true that every layer adds specific functionality, in many systems some 70% to 90% can be considered CRUD-level processing. That goes for the data layer, service implementations, and clients alike. So, there is not just repetition in the horizontal sense (within the layer or tier), but in a vertical sense as well.

As discussed, every layer or tier has its own historical reason for being. In the past, databases made valiant attempts at being application servers as well, but in the end, the industry preferred having a separate application server, based on a 3GL. And for clients, we cannot get around the principal means of building user interfaces: HTML-based browsers and mobile apps. All yield defendable outcomes, but still with a number of consequences.

As long as we do not differentiate between standard CRUD operations and pure business logic, we are fated to convert every piece of data from one representation to another in every layer. Many architectures recognize a data layer for mapping database queries (for example, SQL) to native Java and C# (or other) structures. On top of that, we build another layer that probably processes HTTP/JSON calls and, thus, performs the mapping between JSON and the in-memory structures. While in a web client, we perform conversions between JSON and HTML nodes.

We may also have to repeat code in more than one layer to implement data constraints, such as checking mandatory fields or certain data dependencies. Defining them in the database schema is good for robustness; implementing them a second time in the service layer is advisable, to make sure the service layer copes with them in a neat way; and implementing them for a third time in the UI client can be necessary to let the user know about constraints early in the process of entering data. Owing to this combined horizontal and vertical repetition, every entity and attribute could very well be represented five to tens of times in various fragments of code, all to the detriment of programmer productivity.

Typically, every tier has its own technical implementation, which means that developers might have to be familiar with multiple programming languages and environments. Being a polyglot may give bragging rights in an industry where knowledge is the most valuable asset, but it's not suited for everyone. Many programmers are in a love-hate relationship with SQL. They do not make it a priority to understand all its features; they can use it on the side. This causes many not to fully use the power SQL can offer. Similarly, it may be difficult for an application developer to keep up to date with the most recent developments in HTML. HTML, CSS, JavaScript, and all their frameworks may offer a ton of features, but they also make developing a web client more complex than ever. The question arises whether a full-stack developer is able to deliver sufficient quality on all these terrains. For that reason, this is affecting not just productivity but also quality.

Of course, new concepts, frameworks, and tools promise to ease our lives. NoSQL databases scale better; web frameworks can simplify the handling of HTML screens; and other frameworks may be used to help with the implementation of a service layer. Although to varying degrees of success, some of these techniques do an amazing job.

The problem remaining, however, is that these solutions are by definition partial, because we are so accustomed to thinking in terms of layers and, therefore, typically breed solutions for a given layer (or tier) only. Take the NoSQL movement. This is mostly a database-tier development. AJAX-inspired JavaScript frameworks moved screen rendering from the server to the web browser, but they are not at all concerned with implementation details on the server.

We're faced with a dilemma here. A developer of a new database engine obviously aims to serve the largest audience possible. That makes him/her want to avoid tying into a specific programming language or application server. Instead, he or she will probably go for an API based on something universal, like JSON. Any opportunity to integrate the database within the programming language at the level of the application server is lost by this. With HTTP and JSON, we may have settled a communication protocol and the serialization of data, but that's where the abstraction ends. It certainly is not enough to provide the application server or programming language any notion of the underlying database model.

A communication protocol that does take this extra step could increase the integration between database, application server, and even the client. We can think of exchanging metadata, such that every layer may base its basic read/write (CRUD) functions on the underlying conceptual data model, including, of course, knowledge of the constraints and other logic we need in multiple layers.

This inevitably leads to a chicken-and-egg situation, however. No one is developing such a protocol, because it implies making implementation choices for multiple tiers at once, while the prevailing idea is that every tier has its own separate function and implementation. Therefore, innovations only happen intra-tier: a new JavaScript framework for the client, a new programming language for the application server, or a new database engine that scales better. In a way, the separate tiers of a service-oriented architecture behave like software silos, although vertically separated, instead of horizontally separated.

Although service-oriented architectures have given us so much, they also stand in the way of certain types of innovations. This doesn't mean that the universal aspects of JSON, or XML, for that matter, over HTTP haven't brought a lot. While simple, it is exactly what we needed to escape proprietary, binary, or otherwise limited data exchange. It enabled the integration of every conceivable system in any heterogeneous environment imaginable. For the advocates of open systems, this was a dream come true. And it may remain the lingua franca of so-called open software for long.

This brings us to the distinction we should make between open tiers and open systems. It's not hard to imagine an application environment that is itself heavily integrated yet still very capable of dealing with web services to interact with other systems. We can also imagine a variation in which the communication between tiers is itself still based on an open standard. That would make the tiers of different vendors interchangeable at a higher level than if we limit ourselves to agreeing on JSON and HTTP alone.

A specifically interesting subject in this respect is the relationship between a database and an application server. Database engines were originally designed to be accessible from multiple applications. The goal was to have a large single database in which a company or department could store all its data in one coherent fashion. The advent of the application server, however, started a trend to move all business logic and constraints into the direction of the application server. The application server eventually became the gatekeeper for the underlying database. As a result, in total contrast with the original intent, we ended up connecting each database to a single application server. Interestingly, this puts the *openness* of the database API in a different perspective. It effectively means that a proprietary solution in which the application server and database are better integrated doesn't have to affect the openness of the solution as a whole.

Finally, we must realize that there is a difference between looking at tiers from a conceptual and from a physical perspective. It goes without saying that client and server are always separated from each other over a network. Thus, they form physically separated tiers. But that doesn't mean they have to be viewed as separate, from a conceptual perspective. In the end, an application is a whole. Constraints you define on the level of the data model end up being enforced in the user interface. Again, it's all a matter of *make believe.*

# One Level Too Low

The fact that different tiers have their own implementation, interacting only with a relatively low-level protocol, such as JSON over HTTP, not only has a negative impact on the productivity of application developers, it also causes quality and security issues. Quality, by definition, suffers, if you have to write more code than necessary. If every change to the data model requires multiple changes within multiple tiers, there is a greater chance of introducing bugs.

In addition, the use of multiple programming languages means we sometimes end up mixing them together. Think of assembling an SQL query in a 3GL language, or assembling pieces of HTML, CSS, and JavaScript. This has a number of drawbacks. First, it prevents the integrated development environment (IDE) and compiler from verifying the correctness of that code. It may also mean you have to *escape* pieces of code or data to avoid introducing bugs or even security problems. This is why a strategic snippet of SQL in an input field can be enough to blow up a web site or gain access to far more data than the maker intended.

There are more risks. It is very easy to forget to encode certain parts of a URL. You also have to account for the fact that the user may manipulate URLs. Otherwise, you may introduce security risks. And while JSON may look like a standard, there is no agreement on serialization formats beyond strings and numbers. Dates and timestamps may be serialized in different ways, and it may be that a programmer writes some code to parse JSON in such a way that it breaks when new attributes are added.

What all this boils down to is that, owing to mixing of programming languages and a relatively simple text-based exchange of data, we often have to concern ourselves with low-level aspects, such as serialization, encoding, and escaping. All these things are very error-prone, and they distract us from the actual purpose of the application we're developing.

# Limited by Frameworks

No programming environment can do without frameworks. We do not want to reinvent the wheel constantly, and, therefore, we must contribute to each other's inventiveness. We like to view frameworks as extensions of the core language, but as mentioned previously, it is hard to make that case.

Frameworks come in all shapes and sizes, from small libraries with some convenient extras to complex collections of components that together form a coherent development platform. In whatever form, they are the most explicit and delineated way to combine code from different project teams or individual programmers.

We can divide these frameworks into two categories. On the one hand, there are frameworks with a specific purpose. They may contain specific screens or business logic. The others can be classified as generic. Think of GUI frameworks and object-relational mappers but also more compact things, such as a helper class for dealing with asynchronous communication. Even the string class in a language like C++ falls into this category, because it is part of the C++ Standard Library and, for that matter, not part of the bare language itself.

If basic functionality like this must be added to a language through the use of a framework, this has the benefits of a very clean programming language. But this strategy also has its drawbacks. The fact that the Standard Library was added to C++ at a later stage led to a massive spawning of string classes, all totally incompatible with one another. This model of keeping the language as bare as possible may be well-suited to the purpose of C++, but it is certainly detrimental to the productivity of programmers when building less technical applications.

In addition to that, features that are not part of the language itself are difficult to support within an IDE. They can also be more complex to debug and do not make good use of low-level compiler optimizations.

For example, take a framework that helps you with asynchronous processing for things such as I/O requests. There are multiple ways to implement something like this. Some GUI environments use the user interface event loop, to stay away from multi-threading. Other frameworks, such as Grand Central Dispatch (GCD, from Apple) and Node.js use blocks or callbacks. All these constructs are notoriously hard to debug. That's because the so-called *completion block* you write is invoked seemingly spontaneously, in the sense that the stack-trace rarely reveals the full context of the code you're looking at. Languages that support something like coroutines are at an advantage here, because of such a feature being rooted deeply into the language.

GUI frameworks are handicapped in the same way, because most languages have no native support for a kind of semi-parallel processing (GUI code vs. your own code). This is almost always implemented with the aforementioned event loop. The event loop takes full control over your program, which continuously checks if there are new events (mouse, keyboard) and, in response, updates the screen or invokes program-specific code you authored. The latter is usually implemented as callbacks, which, again, makes it harder to debug the application, the root cause being that the underlying 3GL has no notion of the event loop. It is merely used as a low-level vehicle.

We can observe the same with so-called object-relational mappers. ORM frameworks enable a relational database to disguise itself as a persistent object model. They can never transcend the underlying 3GL, however. This means there can never be a direct relation between the data structures in the language and those in the underlying database model. Instead, you specify a mapping between the two, which is then used either at runtime or by a code generator, to make things work.

There is a slew of problems with this, especially because generating SQL queries based on an object model is not as straightforward as it seems. Navigating from object to object is almost the exact opposite of writing an explicit query that gets all data in one go. ORM frameworks work around this with a lazy loading strategy that only retrieves data when touched, unless specified otherwise. This can easily escalate into lots of small round-trips to the database server, resulting in horrible system performance. As discussed, no framework will ever be able to automatically solve this, simply because within the context of a 3GL, it is not able to perform an analysis of application-specific code. This makes it impossible to predict data access and, therefore, to optimize database requests. In this sense an object-relational mapper only solves part of the impedance mismatch. It does address the way you access the data at a basic level, but it has difficulty bridging the totally different navigational paths that object models and SQL follow.

What we can learn from all these examples is that there is a limit to the degree we can extend the capabilities of a 3GL using only frameworks. Frameworks are able to extend the language with data models and accompanying functions. They may even go beyond that, using callbacks and other clever constructs, but they will never be able to add fundamentally new abstractions to the language. So, if we want to fully integrate database access into a programming language, creating a framework with that purpose is by definition a dead end.

# Human Factors

I've argued that a lot of productivity is lost because, let's say, 80% of the programming we do could have been derived directly from the conceptual data model. Frameworks and 3GLs can't help us, as they have no notion of the persistent data model. And for historical reasons, we utilize three loosely coupled tiers, which has led to isolated evolutionary developments for each. The solution seems obvious: better programming languages and more vertical integration. But why aren't we moving toward that?

Perhaps because it's not immediately apparent how such a vertical integration and accompanying programming language should look. On the other hand, programmers pour tens of thousands of hours into the development of incredibly clever frameworks. If we can tap into this source just a little, we can go a long way.

It may be fear of failure. Initiatives of the past, such as 4GL, CORBA, and object databases, have mostly passed away. SOAP, while still in use, could eventually face a similar fate. Do realize, however, that these solutions all had their own unique problems that were not fundamental to the concept of integration as a whole. 4GL environments were proprietary and were not able to make the leap to Internet technology. SOAP, CORBA, and object databases were needlessly complex, not in the least because they had to be embedded into 3GLs. The potential advantages were negated by the complexity of language neutrality and language mappings, let alone other, more specific, problems haunting these solutions.

However, instead of feeling discouraged by these failures, we can also use them as valuable learning material for future development. Innovation rarely takes a straight path. We must have the guts to take a step back, go back to the drawing board, and combine old insights with new ideas. Software developers especially should never hold back from coming up with and embracing new concepts. We may have to look beyond a few dogmas (the subject of the next chapter), but ideas are aplenty. It is our bread and butter.

Another reason for the reluctance to simplify software development might be that software developers love complexity. Nothing is more satisfying than delving into something and coming out on top, knowing you can now handle more complex problems and that you've become a better software developer. The enormous supply of open source frameworks is the ideal ecosystem to fuel this type of behavior. Maybe that is what prevents us from looking into more fundamental solutions. Every new framework infuses us with the feeling that it will make our lives so much easier. The fact that stacking framework on framework is an inherent source of complexity doesn't scare us enough.

And it is not just software developers themselves who thrive on this complexity. Companies that make development tools or deliver services benefit from a continuous stream of new concepts.

The question is how to break this pattern. Open source projects are often spin-offs of regular software development. Many have thought of something clever in the course of a project. And the brightest among us create something more generally useable and make the time to share this with others. Spin-offs rarely evolve into something like a new programming language or better vertical integration. A spin-off may benefit everybody, but you don't want to suggest building a completely new development environment for your customer. That's just one step too far.

Universities could play a role. Computer scientists certainly think a lot on the subjects of architectures, programming languages, and algorithms. The development of a whole new development environment may be somewhat less obvious, but it is not beyond the realm of possibilities.

Perhaps the industry itself will take up the gauntlet, for example, in the form of a company making its solutions open enough to prevent them from becoming too proprietary. This would not be the first time an isolated initiative developed into a new (de facto) standard. It could create a new industry with different implementations, connectors, shared models, and language extensions.

# Summary

To summarize, we can say that there are two main reasons so few initiatives really contribute to the productivity of application developers. First, 3GLs remain stuck at a certain level of abstraction. Sure, languages do evolve, but more often than not, new features are borrowed from other languages. It is very rare that fundamentally new abstractions are introduced. Regardless, 3GLs have no notion of the conceptual data model of the system as a whole. This is why in every software layer, we redefine more or less the same data model, just in a slightly different form, resulting in a lot of code to exchange data back and forth. A framework may ease the pain, but it can never be a structural solution, as it is unable to really extend a language.

Second, the concept of a three-tier architecture is getting in the way. The separation between database and application server seemed very logical at the same time, but it creates an impedance mismatch, as the database operates with a model very different than that of the application server. And because every database should be able to converse with every application server, the interface between them is as low-level as possible, in the shape of textual SQL statements or JSON messages. Even the communication between UI client and application server would benefit from a more abstract protocol that understands the underlying meta model.

It is always tricky to draw an analogy with another industry, but it is like assembling cars completely from individually designed parts. We combine an arbitrary engine with whatever fuel tank we prefer, mold them onto a hand-built chassis, and add our favorite steering wheel. It pleases us that we are able to combine everything with anything else. The challenge of finding the right combination of parts actually makes us thrive. We like the openness of this approach. However, this openness, in the end, is limited to simple interfaces, such as 12 volts wiring together with some tubes and pipes; nothing like the slick cars of today, with their internal network wiring.

# CHAPTER 4

# Five Dogmas That Hold Us Back

*Technology presumes there's just one right way to do things and there never is.*

—Robert M. Pirsig

We've reached the point where we have to start talking about solutions. Indeed, the second part of this book is dedicated to this. The analyses so far direct us toward a number of solutions. We will have to explore the idea of tighter integration, whether and how we can put the data model center stage, and if we can find a programming language that fits these concepts. There are, however, a few hurdles.

Every analysis and proposal will inevitably lead to some discussion. That is to be expected. But there is more. A number of proposals in this book are diametrically opposed to what some view as fundamental principles of good software architecture. In and of themselves, there is nothing wrong with these principles, but in this book, I take license to return to the drawing board, to explore uncharted territory. Therefore, those fundamental principles may get in the way and become dogmas. Perhaps more so for some than others, however, we cannot avoid examining these (potential) dogmas, one at a time.

© Jos Jong 2019
J. Jong, *Vertically Integrated Architectures*,
https://doi.org/10.1007/978-1-4842-4252-0_4

Many readers will not question the soundness of the so-called three-tier principle, the separation of client, application server, and database. But is this separation mandatory? That is the first dogma we will cast aside. The second is the idea that abstraction layers are not always useful, especially within an information system. The third dogma is the shortcomings of loosely coupling. The fourth concerns monolithic software. The fifth dogma relates to what we can learn from fourth-generation languages (4GLs).

# We Need Three Tiers

Whoever designs an information system today will virtually always start with a three-tier architecture, consisting of a database, application server, and (web) client. But as previously mentioned, in the nineties, a two-tier architecture was commonplace. It all comes down to the separation of application logic from the database. But how fundamental is that?

First, a bit of history. A traditional two-tier environment consisted of a so-called *fat* client and a central database. The business logic was distributed between those two tiers. Given the option to define stored procedures and triggers within the database, it was possible to put some logic close to the data itself, while other logic remained part of the UI client. There seemed to be no need for an additional tier.

This extra tier mainly arose with the advent of web-based applications. Although static HTML could just be hosted on a web server, dynamic HTML had to be rendered based on persistent data. The application server emerged as a solution for this. The business logic from the client tier moved to the application server (this is before AJAX appeared). At the same time, it became less popular to host business logic in the database.

The latter had clear merits. First of all, you did not want to tie your application to a database vendor too much, as with Oracle, in the case of PL/SQL. In addition, it made a lot of sense to write business logic in the same language you use to render your screens.

Along the way, the application server gained an additional role. Traditional databases were never designed to maintain thousands or even millions of user sessions at the same time, which became commonplace on the Internet or in large companies. The application server was, therefore, given the task of distributing all incoming requests among a limited number of connections to the database server, although this did not change the actual load to the database. It was just a workaround for older database architectures.

Originally, database engines were developed with the idea of serving multiple applications. However, with all business logic being moved to the application server, this became increasingly less viable. As a result, the application server became the front end for all communication from and toward other systems. The database transformed into a pure data store for a single application, with the application server guarding all access to that database.

This had another major advantage. If multiple applications are granted direct access to a single database, they will have to migrate along with every incompatible change to the database schema. But now it became possible to support multiple versions of a service, which allows for the bridging between release schedules.

Application servers also made it easier to secure data access, by means of a fine-grained authorization model. Traditional database architectures were not designed with this in mind. They generally only offered options for this at the level of tables and columns, not at the level of user data. For example, when a user's role determines whether he/she may see or not see certain records or attributes.

And finally, the application server could potentially also help with performance, by taking some load of the database. Traditional databases do not scale well horizontally, so removing any kind of processing from it can be beneficial. It's a way of vertical scaling.

Summarizing, the application server alleviates the burden on the database in the following areas:

- Rendering HTML

- Avoiding lock-in on a database vendor

- Managing large amounts of user sessions

- Supporting older clients in case of schema changes

- Fine-grained authorization

- Vertical scaling

The question now is to what extent this list really justifies the separation between database and application server.

Let's start with the last point. The industry has worked hard to improve horizontal scaling of, especially NoSQL, databases. Besides this, both web and mobile clients increasingly are fully featured fat clients that no longer require the application server to render dynamic HTML. It might still be favorable to have some vertical scaling here and there, but it is certainly not a requirement in most cases.

The argument of preventing vendor lock-in is also not fundamental. There is no reason why this argument would be different for database servers than for application servers. We always have to be wary of proprietary solutions, but this is not an inherent property of a database server.

A limit on the number of database sessions is also not fundamentally tied to the concept of a database server, even though this might be true with some existing database implementations. The same is true for authorizations. If we redesign what a database server does and doesn't do, this puts a whole different perspective on both session management and user- and data-level authorization.

The final bridge to cross is how to handle different versions of a database schema. This can be quite a challenging subject, and it will not be solved by magic. But we can also make this a feature of the database. Again, it is not a reason to have a completely separate tier. As will become apparent later in this book, we can actually draw a parallel between schema migrations and the support from older data models toward clients. That will release us from having to write explicit service implementations for most cases.

To conclude, it is a dogma to say we absolutely need three tiers. It's just a matter of design, not a rule set in stone.

# Layers Are Good

Dividing software into separate layers is regarded as one of the most fundamental principles within software engineering. We all know the beautiful schemas vendors create in order to show the modularity of their software. Almost anyone will agree that a layer can abstract away a lot of underlying complexity from the rest of a system. That is why we tend to call them abstraction layers.

The question, however, is whether the layers (and tiers, for that matter) in a typical information system based on a service-oriented architecture (SOA) can be regarded as abstraction layers. We all know the concepts of a data layer, a service layer, and client applications with control and view layers. But how fundamental are these layers to developing an information system?

Of course, it makes sense to put all database access in a separate database or data layer. Owing to the impedance mismatch between databases and third-generation languages (3GLs, such as Java, C#, and others), it is impossible to get things done without a lot of code to glue them together. Every read or update action requires composing a query, supplying it with parameters, and parsing the result afterward. And it is good practice not to mix this up with actual business logic, such as calculations, combining data, etc. So, mainly owing to the impedance mismatch, there seems to be a role for a data layer, in whatever shape.

It could be questioned, however, whether passing around data by itself can be called an abstraction. As said, in a typical SOA architecture, 80% of the code we write in any layer does nothing more than receive the data coming in, before passing it through in a slightly different format. Let's say we store some customer data, such as name and birth date, in a database and later retrieve it for display on the user's screen. We can invent as many ways to represent this data as we like (e.g., fields in a database, in-memory structures, JSON elements, HTML text), but in the end, all these variations still represent the exact same customer data. Imagine we calculate a customer's age, given his/her birth date. In doing this, we add extra data (the age) to the model. But because it is only an addition to the data model, it doesn't replace the original data (the birth date). There may be screens on which the age, rather than the birthdate, is shown, but there will still be screens showing the birth date itself, if only so that its value can be checked and edited.

What this shows us is a fundamental difference between layers in an SOA (or similar) architecture and abstraction layers in a more technical sense. If you write a TCP/IP stack, you will probably use something like the OSI network model to split the intrinsic complexity into different layers. Each layer in such a model handles a piece of this complexity. It is just not easy to manage all the complexity of receiving electronic pulses over a network cable and maintaining a reliable error-corrected connection within a single layer. The OSI layers make sure that the abstraction from one concept to another is taken care of step by step. Each layer solves a problem that the next layer does not need to address: buffering, error correction, reordering packages, sessions, etc.

Another example can be found in the way graphics cards are controlled from within a game. This happens in a number of steps. The core of a game keeps track of the state the game is in. But before any pixels are shown on the screen, a few abstraction layers make sure virtual objects are translated into a 2D image.

Programming languages themselves are also full of such technical abstractions. For example, take the fact that you can create objects in an object-oriented programming language and that these objects are automatically garbage-collected when needed. The mechanism that takes care of this is hidden below the surface. In that sense, this again is a real software abstraction, in this case, something that makes it easier to program in term of objects.

The problem with layers in an information system (SOA-based or not) is that they are a mix of different things. On the one hand, they are involved in technical matters, such as getting access to a database, the exchange of data over network connections, and the conversion of data from one format to another. On the other hand, they contain code that represents actual business logic: evaluating expressions to derive data, processing updates, and checking constraints.

The aforementioned technical aspects are inherently generic by nature. It is only the actual business logic that is unique to the application. If we can capture the generic aspects in the right abstractions, we no longer have to write code for every individual entity, relationship, and attribute to pass data from layer to layer. We could tackle the database impedance mismatch by making persistency part of a programming language, and application-specific business logic could be managed by a generic platform that automatically deals with the communication between tiers.

This way of separating application-specific code from more generic concepts means the traditional multilayer model no longer holds. We can have our own code living conceptually in an abstract world that caters to all necessary technical things under the hood—without building layers.

# Dependencies Are Bad

It can happen to anyone once in a while, to be blamed for introducing an unnecessary dependency within a given piece of software. Preventing certain dependencies is actually the rationale behind a lot of software layers. But how fair is it that dependencies are always portrayed as being so bad? And do extra layers really reduce the number of dependencies? What is a dependency anyway?

There is one type of dependency that we can put aside immediately. We can categorize these as *technically unnecessary* dependencies. As an example, think of indirect dependencies introduced by C and C++ header files. Say you need to include a file to import a given definition, but by doing so, you introduce a dependency on other include files that you actually don't need. This is a very common thing that can happen just because include files include other files, regardless of whether all of those files are relevant in a specific context. Even experienced C and C++ programmers might sometimes lose sleep trying to keep this in check. Unwanted dependencies can lead to problematic circular dependencies or dramatically increased build times. The thing to remember, however, is that they don't have any consequences for the actual code you write. They are just artifacts from the way C and C++ were designed. Modern programming languages are less plagued by this phenomenon. When designing a new programming language, we can avoid this issue from the start.

A reason to put these technically unnecessary dependencies aside is that they are in the mindset of a lot of programmers. This can lead to unwarranted bad judging of dependencies in general, even though they are technically avoidable and have nothing to do with the actual dependencies in the system you're building.

To get back to circular dependencies, they can actually still occur, even when we get rid of all avoidable technical dependencies. That is because data structures are not hierarchical by definition. For example, an object of type A can refer to B, and there is nothing wrong with B directly or indirectly referring back to A. Some compilers are only able to understand this with such things as *forward* declarations. But again, modern compilers are more than capable of dealing with this without trickery. So, we should also see this category of dependencies as a thing of the past.

What we are left with now are intentional dependencies. Think about how data structures refer to each other and the methods invoking other methods. All these dependencies could be classified as meaningful, as long as they exist by design of the application and not for technical reasons. In fact, intentional dependencies are what represent the system itself. After all, the essence of programming is to associate defined data structures with each other and then manipulate them by methods invoking other methods.

Even such things as dynamic languages or other forms of loose coupling cannot avoid these intentional dependencies. They just deal with them at a later stage.

It is fair to say that, by definition, every software system is a collection of intentional dependencies. But then, what exactly is this *problem* with dependencies that we are so often warned about?

The idea that even intentional dependencies are troubling has everything to do with the impact of changes. A change in one part of a system can have a significant impact somewhere else, either in the same system or an external system. But the impact may differ a lot. A single change in a data model may result in the modification of multiple pieces of code, while a change within a class may only impact the implementation of that class itself. For this reason, not all dependencies are as bad as others. Based on the scope of their impact, we could classify them as follows:

1. Limited to a module or class

2. Limited to the system's code base

3. Impact on the code of an associated framework, or vice versa

4.   Impact on an external system due to a remote service

5.   A dependency on the database schema

Before modular and object-oriented programming were introduced, we did not distinguish between categories one and two. But in contrast to spaghetti-like structures, we now only have impact on code outside a module or class, if the API of that module or class changed. That's the point of these concepts. And that is how they help us to build and maintain larger and more complex systems.

Regardless of the distinction, for both categories one and two, we will leave it to the software developer to resolve all related changes. That's because it makes no sense to introduce compiler errors or bugs and have colleagues figure out the consequences of your change.

However, category three is a different story. As a user of a framework, you do not want to be forced to always use the latest version. We develop frameworks to isolate certain data structures and their accompanying logic, sometimes just because it is good to partition a system into separate parts, but oftentimes also to make it available to multiple projects, such as with open source frameworks. But this by definition, of course, decouples the life cycle of such a framework from the projects employing it. The user of a framework will implement and test his or her own system, based on a specific version of that framework. This is actually the biggest raison d'être for most build tools; they manage the use of different versions of frameworks, allowing you to control exactly which version is used in your system.

For category four, the situation is kind of similar. If you invoke a service of another system, you do not want to wake up one morning to find this no longer works, owing to a change in that other system. While many changes are potentially backward-compatible (e.g., certain extensions of the data model), it is probably wise to have a mechanism to indicate the version of the service you are using, for example, by adding a version number to each request. The service implementation can then support one or more older versions, in addition to the current version. As we speak, there is no real standard for doing this. So, this is often a nice bit of artisanal craftsmanship.

Dependencies on the database schema, the fifth category, are perhaps the most visible and impactful dependencies. Of every entity, relationship, and attribute, some aspect will crop up somewhere in the system, sometimes in dozens of locations. After all, the persistent data model represents the state of the system. Because of this, it is reflected everywhere: in data layers, queries, screens, reports, etc. The earlier statement that a system by definition is a collection of intentional dependencies perhaps holds true the most for this category. Database dependencies, however, have their own unique property that we have to account for data migrations. It is not sufficient to perform a schema change on your own development database. As a developer, you may also have to write a script for migration of the production database and all the data in it.

What we can observe here is that there are actually two main categories of dependencies. Categories one and two are purely about changes to a code base. However, for categories three, four, and five, we can't do without some form of build, deployment, or runtime version management. For frameworks (category three), there are a number of conventions, but especially with regard to services (category four) and schema changes (category five), a lot of handcrafting is required, to ensure that different versions can play well together.

So, yes, we do have to cope with dependencies in very specific ways. But let's stop saying that dependencies are *bad*. The essence of a software system is exactly what is reflected by the dependencies between data structures, queries, screens, reports, and business logic that accompany them—as long as they are intentional.

# Monolithic Is Ugly

Classifying a software system as *monolithic* obviously has a negative connotation. Yet, the definition of the word *monolithic* is not as clear-cut. By it, we typically mean something along the lines of "not designed in a modular fashion." But in the context of microservices, people may also mean an application that is deployed as *one big unit*, even though it was built in a very neat and modular way. So, what are we talking about? And is it always that bad?

The term *monolithic* is mainly applied to an application that is becoming less manageable, either owing to increased complexity or its pure size. And this can manifest itself in many ways.

1.  Adapting the code has become increasingly more difficult, for example, because the system has a lot of interwoven logic or a relatively complex design to begin with.

2.  Because of the ever-increasing size, a system has become too large to be maintained by a single team.

3.  The time it takes to build the whole system gets longer and longer.

4.  Deployments are getting more and more complex and take longer.

5.  Booting the application takes increasingly more time.

Let's look at these aspects one at a time. The first point has already been addressed in the preceding "Dependencies Are Bad" section. Dependencies between a data model, screens, and accompanying business logic cannot be avoided, as long as they are there by design. That is what distinguishes intentional dependencies from unnecessary technical dependencies. This means that in an ideal situation, in which a programming environment does not introduce any unnecessary dependencies, we are only left with intentional dependencies. In that sense, we could say that intentional dependencies alone cannot make a system unnecessarily complex. If they do, then it is so by functional design, and that is a whole different subject.

With point two, the question is how large a system should be allowed to grow before it becomes incomprehensible or unmanageable. There are limits to what a single team is able to manage. If those limits are exceeded, or preferably long before this happens, it is time to bring in some systems theory. Maybe it possible to view part of the system as a subsystem, either based on ownership, functionality, or the domain model. It might even be possible to assign one of those subsystems a central role to be shared by multiple other systems.

Looking at subsystems in this way, *too big* and *too small* cannot be seen as absolute terms, in the same way as there is no set limit for how large a department within a company should be allowed to grow. That would also depend on the context and details such as the specific role of that department, its responsibilities, the size of the organization as a whole, the span of control of the management, etc. In this respect, it is interesting to refer to Conway's Law,[1] which states that "Any organization that designs a system (defined broadly) will produce a design whose structure is a copy of the organization's communication structure." This actually makes perfect sense in many situations, especially from the viewpoint of ownership.

Points three, four, and five are about build, deployment, and runtime performance. Ideally, these are not things you want to worry about as an application developer. So, if we think about a totally new development platform, and that is the angle of this book, then these have to be among the considerations. It is a matter of smart integral design. If build, deployment, and runtime performance all scale very well, regardless of the size of the system, there is now reason to call a system monolithic.

---

[1]Melvin E. Conway, "Conway's Law," www.melconway.com/Home/Conways_Law.html.

It is very tempting to dogmatically label as monolithic every system that is a little bigger or more integrated, but how fair that is really depends on the context. With a development environment that scales well in every aspect, the size of a (sub)system should mostly be an organizational topic.

# 4GL Is Dead

A whole generation was raised with the idea that 4GLs would eventually supersede 3GLs, making the life of programmers a whole lot easier, or even that they would become redundant, because end users would be able to do the programming themselves. The next generation learned little about 4GLs or only vaguely remembers having heard about them during their studies, knowing that it never became a relevant success. But are 3GLs really the highest-level programming languages we can attain?

In the nineties, the term *4GL* was related to such concepts as rapid application development (RAD) and computer-aided software engineering (CASE). Although there were no strict boundaries between all these developments, there was certainly a clear theme behind them: programming at a higher level, resulting in fewer lines of code to write.

The general sentiment today is that 4GL is a thing of the past—a failed experiment, a dead end that we have to avoid like a plague. But this is a far too grim and limited view.

First, forget about the term *4GL*. It is intended here to refer to any software development tool that requires less or minimal coding, in the broadest sense, either by employing higher-level languages, domain-specific languages (such as screen definitions), or partly by configuration. And although this includes the already mentioned CASE and RAD tools, this also covers their modern counterparts, including the following:

- Low-code and no-code development platforms

- High-productivity application platforms as a Service (HPaPaaS)

This market is a bit under the radar for most hard-core software developers, but it has actually been growing for some years now. Forrester estimates the market for low-code platforms to reach beyond $10 billion in the year 2020 (see Figure 4-1).[2]

**Projected low-code development platform market growth**

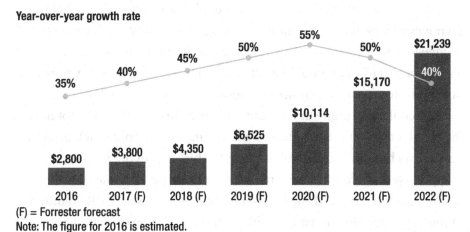

*Figure 4-1.* *Forrester's low-code platforms forecast (US$ billions)*

Apart from a lot of small players, two of the biggest in this market today are

- Mendix, established 2005, 400 employees[3]

- OutSystems, established 2001, 600+ employees[4]

---

[2]John R. Rymer, et al., "Vendor Landscape: A Fork in the Road for Low-Code Development Platforms," www.forrester.com/report/Vendor+Landscape+A+Fork+In+The+Road+For+LowCode+Development+Platforms/-/E-RES137578, July 31, 2017.

[3]Wikipedia, "Mendix," https://en.wikipedia.org/wiki/Mendix, 2018.

[4]Wikipedia, "OutSystems," https://en.wikipedia.org/wiki/OutSystems, 2018.

We should also not forget that OpenEdge ABL, which started its life as
Progress 4GL in 1984, is still alive and kicking. And another one to mention
is WinDev. This is kind of an outsider, but this tool from PC Soft has
existed since 1984. Its 23rd edition was released in 2018, and it seems to be
relatively popular within French and Brazilian markets, with well-attended
conferences.

Another misconception that many people have about 4GL is that we
do not need a better programming language, because of the advanced 3GL
frameworks that we have today. However, as discussed before, frameworks
can never add fundamental new abstraction to a 3GL. That's why they can
never fully free us from certain code repetition and low-level coding.

You could also argue that we don't need 4GL because we do not have
the problems it is trying to address. But attempts to simplify such things as
service call handling and database access (think about object-relational
mappers) tell a different story. In a way, every framework that tries to
simplify such technical things as asynchronous processing, URL handling,
or low-level security indicates a certain omission in the development
environment we work with.

There is also this idea that the higher level a language is, the more it
has to be restricted to a specific domain. Indeed, a lot of the traditional
4GL-like tools, then and now, were designed with a typical business-type
of information system in mind. But that was, of course, where most of
IT was practiced. The Internet didn't even exist yet. We must remember,
too, that every development platform has its limitations in this sense. It
is not worth trying to build a device driver in Java, let alone developing a
high-performance game. Perhaps the development of real-time industrial
applications will always be done with different tools than those used for
information systems. But on the other hand, almost every system, to a
certain extent, is an information system. Even the tiniest piece of software
receives data, stores it, and has ways to query that data, or share it over
a network. There is no apparent reason we cannot use the same well-

thought-through concepts for most applications. It is just the extremes, such as certain high-performance applications and such languages as C and C++, that are the exceptions that prove the rule.

This leaves us with the subject of openness and connectivity. One of the issues with 4GL-like tools in the nineties was figuring out how to integrate them in a heterogeneous software environment. But there are, of course, lots of ways to escape that today. We can connect anything now with JSON over HTTP, something that did not exist in the previous century.

So, maybe 4GL is not the hippest technology anymore, but is the concept behind it dead? Certainly not, if we look at the market of low-code and HPaPaaS development. Apart from that, there has always been an appetite to simplify software development. We just have to figure out a more general-purpose, universal, and, it is to be hoped, less proprietary solution than the market is producing today. That is precisely the focus of this book.

# CHAPTER 5

# The Solution: Vertical Integration

*A software developer's proper role was to create tools that removed the need for software developers with proper design, the features come cheaply. This approach is arduous, but continues to succeed.*

—Dennis Ritchie

After all the problem analysis to this point, it is finally time to go back to the drawing board and think about solutions. So that's what I am going to do from this chapter onward.

I started this book by identifying the different problems that have caused developer productivity and quality to stagnate for so long. From the historic perspective offered in Chapter 2, you learned that there are actually good reasons why we do the things the way we do. However, historic reasons cannot be sufficient to keep doing things in a certain way. Sometimes, the only way to progress is to take a step back—back to the essence of data modeling and programming, in this case.

The main conclusion that we can draw from the analysis in Chapter 3 is that the separate layers and tiers we invented may solve certain issues, but they also created a fragmented world in which every tier is implemented in its own completely distinct way. Clients, application servers, and databases all live in their own world with different concepts, languages, and runtime environments. This is what leads to the duplication of the application's data model in multiple formats and duplication of certain business logic.

© Jos Jong 2019
J. Jong, *Vertically Integrated Architectures*,
https://doi.org/10.1007/978-1-4842-4252-0_5

Even worse, this setup creates an impedance mismatch between application server and database and a lowest-common-denominator solution for interfacing between client and server, such as JSON over HTTP. In addition, all this makes it impossible to establish a clear separation between standard read/write (CRUD) actions and pure business logic. That is one of the reasons why it is so difficult to automate CRUD operations, forcing us to write tons of code that otherwise could have been deduced from the data model.

This is where the title of this book comes in: *Vertically Integrated Architectures*. Vertical integration, in the sense of aligning tiers with each other or even merging tiers together, gives us a lot of potential to solve the issues mentioned. It can bring concepts together again, thereby lowering impedance mismatch and reasons for duplication.

The obvious starting point is to combine the application server and database again, as discussed in the "We Need Three Tiers" dogma section of Chapter 4. However, that's not going to solve anything by itself. Can we combine the database data model with the programming data model? What type of programming language do we need? How do we interface with such a combined server? And why would all this be different from other attempts to obviate the same problems, such as two-tier development environments in the nineties, MDD code generation, and today's low-code environments?

# A Vertically Integrated Architecture

Merging the application server and database server can simplify a lot of things, but only if we overcome a few challenges. The first challenge has to do with data modeling. The so-called impedance mismatch between the code we write and the database is owing to the fact that our programming language and database use completely different concepts to model data. Trying to talk in terms of objects against a set of tables is like trying to push a square peg through a round hole. As explained before, even object databases and ORMs cannot fully solve this impedance mismatch. The reason behind this is quite fundamental: it is because both are trying to glue persistency into a 3GL (third-generation programming language) that fundamentally is only concerned with in-memory operations.

But there is a solution to this issue. Take, for example, in-database languages such as Oracle's PL/SQL. Because PL/SQL stored procedures live inside the database, the compiler and query optimizer can analyze the query and update statements against the database model (the table definitions) and even incorporate data statistics, to determine the best access paths. This is what 3GLs will never be able to do, because they're not aware of data persistency, let alone the fact that they will never be able to predict upcoming queries and updates to prevent unnecessary network round-trips (the previously discussed lazy loading problem). This means that we can only make this perform if we, as programmer, decide what query to execute at what moment. But that, again, stands in the way of automatically deducing a lot of code from the data model. It is all related.

It is not that the relational model has some magical properties that makes it easier to optimizer queries. We do not have to stick with the relational theory, for that matter. It is just a good example of how code living in the database can be analyzed against the data model and data statistics to optimize its execution. In theory, we can do that with every language that expresses itself in terms of the underlying persistent data model.

Bringing together application logic and data persistency also means it is easier to deduce general read/write behavior from the underlying database schema. Just as with any existing database engine, we can define a generic interface that clients or external systems can use to communicate with the system, in terms of its data model. This can all be achieved without having to write specific service implementations for these standard operations.

But this is where we can, and must, learn from the nineties' two-tier era. One of the reasons to create a third tier, the application server, was to decouple the database from clients and external systems. As discussed, this decoupling is mostly needed to isolate schema changes. It can be difficult or impossible to force a client or other system to follow every data model change that we make. This means that without any way in which we can be backward-compatible with older clients, it is impossible to implement certain data model changes. This can potentially bring development to a halt, especially with a lot of systems connected to one another.

This sounds as if the whole idea of deducing CRUD operations from the data model will never work; however, that is, of course, unless we figure out how to be backward-compatible without having to write explicit services implementation. That is precisely what I am going to discuss in the coming chapters. You will see how we can use functional-style schema mappings to specify how we want to migrate data from one version of a model to another version of the same model. The server can use that to automatically adapt itself to older clients. You will also learn that there is actually a direct parallel between being backward-compatible and database migrations.

Because this idea is the opposite of explicitly written service implementations, I will call it *implicit services* from now. This concept has a lot of benefits. It means that we can design a generic database-like API to access the server. After defining a data structure, we can immediately start entering (test) data and building a client to access and manipulate that data. This, of course, assumes that we give the client full control of what data to access, which is the total opposite of a service-oriented architecture (SOA). But you will see later that this eventually has a lot of benefits. I will also go beyond the typical one-to-one entity-based CRUD services, as with a typical REST interface. Instead, I will define a fully featured query interface that enables clients to read all data to load a screen with a single network call.

Obviously, we need some sort of authorization control, especially with external clients. But given the right conceptual data model, we can use that as a foundation for a fine-grained authorization model that can both be based on the data structure and data- or user-specific authorization rules.

We can use implicit services in multiple ways. By making them available in a generic readable JSON-over-HTTP form, we can have any web, mobile, or external system access and update data on the server. Vertical integration, however, doesn't have to stop by combining the application server and database. We can also create a client environment that understands the server-side data model, for example, with web and mobile frameworks that can execute screen definition defined in terms of the conceptual data model on the server. Such clients will be able to automatically generate the implicit services requests required to handle screen refreshes and commit data triggered by user actions, but having metadata accessible from a client also creates opportunities for more generic tools to manage, test, and repair data, just as we do with today's generic database tools.

Figure 5-1 illustrates the differences between a mainstream SOA and a vertically integrated architecture. We can see that with SOA, each tier has a totally different programming environment that also dictates the programming language to use for the application-specific code in that tier. A vertically integrated architecture (VIA), on the other hand, consists of a runtime environment that serves as a generic backbone for the whole architecture. As a result, a data model, business logic, and screen definitions can all live in the same conceptual world, completely separate from the technical details of the platform.

**A Typical Service-Oriented Architecture**    **A Vertically Integrated Architecture**

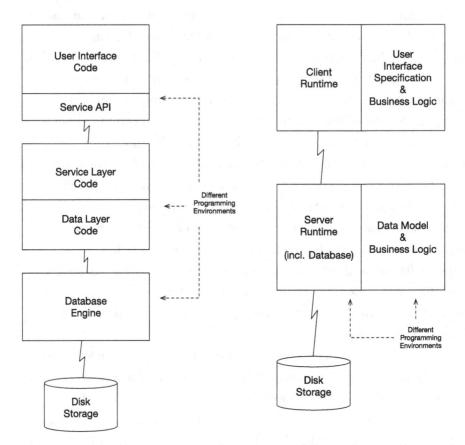

***Figure 5-1.*** *SOA vs. VIA*

In a way, it's a 90-degree shift. While in SOA the tiers attempt to abstract the application into layers, in a VIA, the abstraction lies in a runtime that takes care of the generic behavior, to create a conceptual world dedicated to application development.

The VIA philosophy proposed here is based on three pillars:

- A unified conceptual data model that serves as database schema, programming data model, and client-side data model

- Implicit services as a generic API for client access

- A persistence-aware programming language to write pure business logic, constraints, update procedures, and authorization rules

These three pillars will be the subject of the next chapters, but let's start with an introduction to all three.

# A Unified Conceptual Data Model

In a way, a unified conceptual data model plays the same role as an entity model within a model driven development (MDD) environment. There is one major difference, however. Instead of being used to generate 3GL code, it will be a live runtime-available meta model. Later, you will see how this is key to making things work in a vertically integrated environment with implicit services and an accompanying programming language. To name one thing, having a runtime meta model makes it feasible to manage different versions of the data model, which, as said, is one of the key design goals to make implicit services work.

The conceptual data model is kind of the foundation for everything else, in the sense that apart from being the database schema, it is also the foundation on which we can build business logic. It is the basis for implicit services, and we can refer to it from screen definitions (in the sense of binding screen elements to data model elements and queries). But what does a unified conceptual model, or, rather, meta model, look like?

It should first and foremost be a purely *conceptual* model. It is entirely possible that the serialization of a data set over TCP/IP is very different than that of the same data set stored in a database. In an in-memory cache, the storage format may be different again. A runtime will be able to automatically handle all these differences, as long as there is a single unequivocal implementation-independent description (the *conceptual* model) of the underlying data model for that data set. Let's discuss a few options, to get the full picture.

We are looking for something that can pursue the role of both a database schema and a programming model at the same time. As with MDD, there is one obvious candidate: entity-relationship (ER) modeling, and I will indeed get back to that in a minute. But let's first look at a few database models, for comparison.

The relational model sounds like quite a conceptual model, with its separation between the definition of a model, its internal implementation, and external representation. However, there is an issue with the relational theory. That's because it doesn't treat relationships between entities as first-class citizens. Entities and attributes can be translated into tables and columns. But to model the relationships between entities, you have to fall back to the principle of foreign keys, using attributes. (Note: Contrary to common belief, the word *relation* refers to entities, not to the relationships between them.) Codd later realized this shortcoming, and in his so-called RM/T publication,[1] he introduced the concept of *associations* (in addition to a lot of other things), to try to fix this omission. This, however, never substantiated into the world of relational databases. In SQL, it never became possible to refer to a relationship (association) by means of a name or something similar. Instead, we still rely on where-clauses, comparing key values to indicate what relationships

---

[1]E. F. Codd, "Extending the Database Relational Model to Capture More Meaning," *ACM Transactions on Database Systems* (TODS) 4, no. 4, December 4, 1979, pp. 397–434.

we want to incorporate in a query. This indirect way of interacting with relationships can make it more difficult to read queries and, for that matter, more difficult to judge their correctness. It also sits in the way of a pure conceptual way of thinking, because it literately exposes the way a relationship is implemented. Even the smartest database optimizations always have to deal with the primary and foreign key columns as defined, giving them less freedom to choose a totally different implementation. In addition, foreign keys are no solution for many-to-many relationships, for which we have to define separate linking-tables, again making it more difficult to understand queries.

Would JSON documents be a candidate, as in so many NoSQL databases? Although, strictly speaking, it is a type of data serialization, one could deduce an underlying conceptual model from it. It is hierarchical, in the sense that there is a root that everything falls below. Arrays may be viewed as multiple records of the same type and, therefore, as entities. And dictionaries are used as key-value pairs, to represent attribute values. Because an attribute, in turn, may be an array (list) or dictionary (record), it is possible to build deeply nested hierarchies of data with one-to-one and one-to-many relationships. We could categorize a JSON-document-based database as a collection of hierarchical mini-databases.

Unfortunately, this model has a lot of limitations as well. Data models are not necessarily hierarchical. So, it can very well happen that we need the help of foreign keys to cross-reference nodes within a document or across multiple documents, as with the relational model. The requirement to divide data models into clusters of data, the JSON documents, is also not a very conceptual thing to do. This means that practical and technical matters get reflected in the way we manipulate and query the data in these documents, which can get in the way with later refactorings of the model.

Another potential candidate for the unified data model we are looking for is an object model. Particularly with an object-oriented programming language, this would fit perfectly. It is exactly what object databases tried to do. We could manage the object model's state with the database engine and build business logic in terms of objects, by calling their methods. As in many modern object-oriented programming languages, we could get rid of the tedious job of having to define setters and getters with the concept of *properties.*

There is, however, one big issue with object modeling: it totally lacks the idea of relationships between objects. We manage to work around that by using collection classes, but collections are just objects, in the end. They are not first-class citizens, meaning that with the exception of some *iterator* syntactic sugar, programming languages do not know what's happening inside a collection. That is especially a disadvantage with persistent data. With more complex database queries, we want the database to be able to understand the data model and calculate the most efficient way to access data, for example, by choosing to use an index or by processing whole sets of data in parallel. That becomes a problem if we can only represent relationships with collections that we can iterate through.

In the end, of course, every form of data modeling has its pros and cons. As discussed, a lot of database modeling techniques have very limited or indirect support for relationships. Things such as foreign keys and collection classes are kind of technical workarounds that do not really fit into the idea of a conceptual data model. On the other end, the fact that we associate methods to objects in an object database model makes it an ideal candidate to fit into an object-oriented programming language. The relatively simple and hierarchical structure of JSON documents can simplify a lot of things. The set-oriented approach of the relational model led to an extremely universal and optimizable query language that we call SQL.

Now let's look at what ER modeling can do for us. The ER model has been studied extensively, extended, and described. Since Chen's first formalized form,[2] it has come a long way, with lots of variations and

---

[2]Peter Pin-Shan Chen, "The Entity-Relationship Model—Toward a Unified View of Data," *ACM Transactions on Database Systems* (TODS) 1, no.1, March 1976, pp. 9–36.

different schema notations, and it even got a place in the Unified Modeling Language (UML) schema set as UML data modeling. In the end, however, the biggest difference between all of these variations is the way we draw the lines that represent relationships, not a big thing to bother about, really. The essence here is that ER modeling provides a good conceptual foundation for every imaginable model. It has a clear concept of relationships, and some variations even include such things as subtyping and ownership.

To reach the goal of a unified conceptual data model, we can learn from both ER and database modeling. Obviously, the ER model is a good conceptual basis, but a bit of object-orientation would be nice, to integrate the data model into a programming language. The clear compositional (ownership) aspects of JSON documents and the set-oriented approach of the relational model can also be useful things to throw into the mix.

In Chapters 6 and 7, you will see how we can combine these concepts into a single unified conceptual data model that can be a persistent model and programming model at the same time. You will then also learn how the way we query data cannot be separate from the way we model data.

# Implicit Services

Given a unified conceptual data model, we can establish generic read/ write behavior to access the actual data with what we call implicit services. Let's see what this would be like in practice.

Services in a traditional SOA architecture can be regarded as pre-baked queries. That is the core of the matter. Provided we take care of a few provisions, it is much more flexible if we can specify our queries directly from within a user interface or external system, seemingly as if we had direct access to the database. The fear this evokes with application developers is, as discussed, significant. It's understandable, from a historic perspective, but it is absolutely not a fundamental restriction. That's because we can decouple the client and server-side model version with an integrated schema versioning system. To prevent any unwanted data access, we could integrate a fine-grained authorization system inside the server engine.

With an SOA service, a request consists of the name of the service and some parameters. Instead, with an implicit service, a client indicates exactly what entities, attributes, and relationships it wants to inquire about. If we supplement this with features from a persistence programming language, we can make it into a full-blown query language that allows for the expression of every conceivable query. It no longer is a service layer, but a general query engine that can be accessed with a universal query language.

At its core, this sounds no different than any other existing database query language. It is not a totally new concept, of course. So-called *backend as a service* (BaaS) products have been moving in the same direction. However, later, you will see that with the right conceptual model and a different look on service granularity, this concept will go way further than any other database query language.

Although with implicit services standard read/write operations come out of the box, they certainly do not have to be limited only to accessing the plain data model. By making it possible to associate functions with entities, as in an object model, we can define server-side business logic that a client can refer to from within a service request. Functions in this sense act as views on the data. By making it possible to refer to any combination of both data elements and functions in a single service request, the client can retrieve any set of data it wants, with a single network round-trip.

Unlike a lot of contemporary databases, such as SQL, implicit services can fully support hierarchical queries and hierarchical results. A client would be able to specify exactly which relationships to follow and which attributes it wants or does not want to be returned. You can even add filters at different nested levels, for example, to retrieve only the last five orders of a customer, then only the order lines and corresponding product data for the most recent order.

By the way, all this is not about a specific serialization format for service requests. As with the data model itself, it all starts with a conceptual approach that tells us the semantics. We can then define one or two different ways to serialize such requests and accompanying responses, for example, one for clients that fully integrate with the VIA client/server architecture, and a second one that exposures a JSON variant for external systems.

Most of the preceding applies to data retrieval. But we can, of course, also call a service to update data. There is, however, a good reason to keep read and write services apart. While a read service request is basically just a set of expressions, an update could take the form of a script. Although both read and write services can call server-side methods, we want to make sure that read services do not call methods that update data. That's a good reason to strictly distinguish between functions (read-only) and procedures (update methods).

As functional programming languages teach us, there is a lot we can do knowing that a given function is idempotent and without side effects. It makes it possible to combine and stack queries and force any thinkable optimization, without consequences to the actual result. This is no different than established databases that do not execute a query in a verbatim way. They also first analyze and reshuffle the elements within a query, taking into account nested views and functions, before determining the most optimal query plan.

# A Persistence-Aware Language

Although implicit services make it unnecessary to write boilerplate code for CRUD operations, we still need a language to write business logic, in the sense of procedures, functions, constraints, and other server-side logic (potentially also for the client side, but that's a subject that I will skip for now). So, the challenge is to define such a language that naturally speaks in terms of the underlying unified data model, in other words, is persistence-aware.

Persistence awareness of programming languages is certainly not a new phenomenon. I already discussed how object databases made 3GLs go along, sort of, with database access. SQL extensions such as Oracle's PL/SQL are examples of database access and programming fully integrated with each other. With 4GLs, database integration was self-evident. But apart from all these solutions having their problems, they all do not fit the unified ER-like data model proposed here.

What we need is a modern, clean, and optimizable programming language in which accessing persistent data is not an afterthought but the *number-one* abstraction. The proposed unified data model closely resembles an object model approach, extended with full conceptual support for relationships. So, the question is how we can give the filtering of objects, traversing relationships, and various other forms of data retrieval and data transformation a prominent position in such a language?

We could start by using collection classes, as we know them from object-oriented programming languages. Many languages and frameworks already support such functional operations as filter, map, and reduce for querying data from collections. "Problem solved," you may say. But this is where it gets interesting: why do we need these collection classes in a programming language in the first place? By definition, programming is something you do on collections of objects. It is pointless to build a software system in which you can store the data of a single customer. The fact that you may have multiple records with the same structure is the very essence of developing software. Software frees us from repetitive tasks, and repetition is about processing *more of the same.*

With the *everything is an object* mantra, object-oriented languages defined alternatives to arrays, in the guise of collection classes. Granted, in many languages, arrays are very limited in terms of features. In these cases, collection classes are far more flexible, universal, or just safer alternatives.

This approach, however, destined collections to be second-class citizens. If we want to elevate database access to a higher level of abstraction, we should address this first. For a compiler, a collection implemented in the form of an instance of a class is nothing more than any other object. This prevents a compiler from getting the bigger picture, in the sense of what sets of data are being processed in which way. So, even though a compiler could optimize a lot of low-level 3GL operations, it will never be able to reveal the purpose of iterating a certain collection within a piece of code. Given also that this only happens in memory, all this is very irreconcilable with a more database-centric vision.

In the end, the problem is in the term *object-oriented*. In an object-oriented language, the manipulation of objects in memory is the foremost data abstraction. If we want to design a more database-oriented language, we have to bet on a set-oriented language.

The idea of a set-oriented language is not new. SETL (SET Language)[3] is an example of such a language. For some reason, however, the concept never took off in that form. SQL is very much set-oriented, but without extensions, it is not a programming language on its own. There are, of course, elements of set orientation in some, especially dynamic, programming languages, but they are still very bound to the 3GL memory model.

It's all about finding the right concepts. What we need is an abstraction in which we can query and manipulate data in terms of objects, attributes, and relationships in any way we want, while allowing the compiler and runtime to independently decide how to actually perform those actions. Referring to a property, then, no longer implies the literal retrieval of the corresponding value, as it would with getter and setter methods. Navigating relationships becomes a more readable way to express joins. Whether filtering data by a filter condition occurs in memory or during disk I/O (for example, with the help of an index) can be left up to the optimizer.

---

[3]SETL, https://setl.org/.

# Challenges

Nothing comes for free. So, let's look at the challenges that come with the aforementioned ideas.

The first challenge is concerned with performance. The idea of vertical integration is that the compiler and runtime are given enough information to help us with this, with both network optimizations and disk access optimizations.

Network optimization is mostly about limiting the number of round-trips. That's where the main costs reside. Therefore, this will be one of the main optimizations I will touch on in Chapter 8 on implicit services. It will show you how implicit services are a big help for network performance, because they relieve us from the so-called fine-grained vs. course-grained design dilemma.

While this *perfect granularity* (as I call it) is a new thing, there is actually a ton of knowledge available on how to optimize disk access. I am talking about query optimizers. For most of us, their intelligence is completely hidden, but they are true marvels, especially in SQL databases. The novel thing here is that we will have to apply this approach to a programming language that is way more general-purpose than an SQL query. We suddenly have to view a piece of code as if it were a query, including all function calls and whatever external code it invokes. But there is a solution to this problem. While most compilers apply a massive number of optimizations to their memory-focused operations, we can stretch this to the realm of persistency. The way to do that is to regard the code to be executed as a single massive query that can be analyzed and reshuffled as any normal database query. As a result, the one-by-one compilation of individual source files into executable code no longer fits the bill. I dive into the details of this technique in the chapter about persistence-aware programming.

Another very interesting, but challenging, research and design area is that of integrated version management. In current architectures, this is virtually always done by hand. Developers write migration scripts for databases, assign version numbers to frameworks, and utilize version numbers in service APIs, in order to support an older version of that API. If we delve into this, we will see that all these things are more related than you might think. Supporting older versions of an API and converting an old database to a newer schema is conceptually not that different. The version control of a data model and accompanying source code are also tightly related. It is difficult to manage that relationship with individual files, such as with Git. Perhaps, above all, we should realize that metadata, method signatures, and pieces of source code, in the end, are all data themselves. If we fundamentally rethink how to deal with historical data in a database, we can apply a lot of (or maybe even all) the same principles to metadata.

In addition to all these technical challenges, there are plenty of nontechnical ones as well. For evidence of this, we need only cast a glance at the past.

4GL and RAD suffered not only from the fact that their concepts didn't fit well within the big Internet revolution at the time but also because every vendor dreamt up its own solution. Every 4GL/RAD environment was put together completely differently and generally employed its own proprietary programming language. A so-called *vendor lock-in* was inevitable. Even though there certainly was a lot of enthusiasm for some of these tools, this did not turn out to be very sustainable.

We can learn a lesson from that. Unless in a sub-niche market, to be successful means being open, in the sense of setting or supporting open standards. It helps organizations to secure their investments in a platform, while at the same time creating a market for multiple parties to implement their own specific implementations of parts of the platform. Standardization would be very welcome for both the programming language and the APIs between the different modules, such as GUI, server, and development environment. A de facto standard could be a good starting point, but any form of standardization very likely will be a critical success factor in establishing the VIA architecture, as proposed in this chapter.

To be as generic-purpose as possible should be another design goal. Sure, the focus of this book is on information systems, but although such things as games, device drivers, and aircraft operating systems are of a totally different league, we should avoid to delineate these markets too sharply. Languages that are not 3GL quickly tend to be called *domain-specific*. That seems to suggest that if a language has a higher level of abstraction, we suddenly need to choose which industry it is targeted toward. There is, however, no relationship between better abstractions and application areas, as long as these abstractions are general purpose by themselves. It is true that 4GL and RAD platforms mainly targeted information systems, and all of these environments might have had different focuses (such as performance, certain types of industries, or others), but all that is not a fundamental attribute of a higher language abstraction. With all the arguments and propositions in this book, you should be able to develop a language that is sufficiently generic and broadly applicable.

Let me end by saying a few words about complexity vs. simplicity. Admittedly, a VIA architecture, as proposed in this book, implies a lot of complex development challenges, because of its ambitious deviation from familiar architectures. But we should first and foremost distinguish between intrinsic complexity and unnecessary complexity. The latter may be the result of bad design, poor choices, or a fetish for complexity itself. Or it could be due to stacking one complexity onto another, as happens when you glue a lot of existing techniques together. Just throwing a lot of simple solutions at a problem could very well end up being way more complex than formulating a few well codesigned solutions with a good foundation. That's why we need to go back to the drawing board as much as required, reject every existing solution that doesn't fit in well, and have a continuous focus on simplicity in every detail of specification and implementation.

Considering intrinsic complexity, we should distinguish between internal and external complexity. Nobody will claim that developing a new development environment, application server, or database engine is easy (high internal complexity). It's just an expert's job. It always was, and it will be forever. We will have to live with that. It's the price we should be willing to pay to significantly simplify the life of the hundreds of thousands of application developers who will use this potential piece of art to build real applications.

## Summary

A vertically integrated architecture (VIA) can relieve us from an enormous amount of code plumbing. By making the application environment responsible for all basic operations, such as querying data, exchanging data over a network, and the rendering of screens, application developers can focus on the things that really matter: functionality and quality.

In this chapter, I discussed the following essential pillars for such a development environment:

- A unified conceptual data model that serves as database schema, programming data model, and (optionally) client-side data model

- Implicit services that serve as a generic service API

- A persistence-aware programming language to write pure business logic, constraints, update procedures, and authorization rules

The gist of this approach is that we stop investing in partial per-tier solutions and instead abstract the entire data flow through a system. This also implies giving the integrated programming language a humbler role. Humble, in the sense that the compiler or interpreter no longer translates our source code to (virtual) hardware instructions, doing only memory manipulation. Instead, all code in which we access data is to be interpreted by the compiler and runtime, as kinds of super queries, to either result in a single network call from client to server or the least amount of disk I/O within the server itself.

In this vision, a separation between application server and database only results in undesirable additional complexity. This book, therefore, can be regarded as an appeal to the reawakening of two-tier architectures, albeit in a completely modernized way, of course.

If we go so far as to also fully integrate client-side development into this vision, we can even extend the idea to a one-tier solution. Even though client and server will, of course, always be different nodes on the network, we would no longer have to specify exactly what code runs where. We will then have achieved a physical two-tier environment driven by a one-tier conceptual view of an application. This is a separate option, however. We will get back to this when I talk about user interfaces, at the end of this book.

Admittedly, ideas on paper still don't make a working system. The goal of this book, however, is just to create awareness and to inspire— awareness of the fact that we have reached the ceiling with so many of today's concepts and the inspiration to come up with a fresh approach to vertical integration.

And, as stated, we are not going to leave things there. In the coming chapters, I will delve into the details of each of the previously cited three pillars of the VIA philosophy.

# CHAPTER 6

# The Art of Querying

*Simplicity does not precede complexity, but follows it.*

—Alan Perlis

With this chapter, you reached this book's second half, which is dedicated entirely to fleshing out the details of the vertically integrated architecture (VIA) outlined in Chapter 5. This distinguishes it from the first half, which advocated the need for a different approach. This second part is meant to provide inspiration. After having identified the problems and reflected and argued about them, the focus now shifts to the solutions I propose.

Obviously, the ultimate way to prove a new approach is to develop a working software product. I will not attempt to detail every aspect of such a product. This book is not intended for that purpose. Still, there is a lot to say about the consequences, possibilities, and challenges that arise from striving toward such a far-reaching form of vertical integration. For example, it is all well and good to say that the access to the database must and can be integrated into a programming language, but the big question is how that would look in practice. Implicit services may be a sound idea, but it is interesting to see how an actual request to a server would look.

I will address all these subjects, with concrete examples, technical deliberations, points of attention, interesting insights, and also pointing out the challenges to be met with certain aspects, not, as stated, in the sense of a detailed design, but still as a solid base for discussions, pilot projects, and real-world implementations.

© Jos Jong 2019
J. Jong, *Vertically Integrated Architectures*,
https://doi.org/10.1007/978-1-4842-4252-0_6

The most essential pillars of what we call a VIA architecture have been mentioned earlier.

- A unified conceptual model

- Implicit services

- A persistence-aware programming language

While each can be studied separately, it is because of their tight integration that these subjects are fully connected. You can't view a programming language in which you can directly access the underlying database separate from how that database is modeled. It matters whether the database is relational, hierarchical, object-oriented, graph-based, or documented-oriented. Every query or expression in which you consult data reflects the choice of a certain meta model. Because queries play an important part both in the programming language and with implicit services, the meta model and the accompanying query language are the foundations on which the rest of the VIA architecture is built.

Because of this, I will begin part two with a proposal for a suitable conceptual data model, including a perspective on how we can interact with that model. I do this in two chapters. In the first, I will mainly focus on querying data, and in the subsequent chapter, I will look at data manipulation and its influence on the meta model.

You will see especially that the way in which we model and query relationships is an important consideration. Many database concepts and, therefore, query languages seem to have been built around entities and attributes (in terms of ER modeling), with relationships being a kind of second-class citizen. Queries are about finding, filtering, and transforming entities, but most often in conjunction with their relationships to other entities. In this chapter, you will see what we can learn from natural language in this respect, still only to be applied to a formalized language, but with the aim of making queries as compact and readable as possible.

# It's All About Relationships

To fully integrate a query language within a programming language, we have to start by getting rid of any unnecessary differences between the two. We're better off striving for fusion than integration. Only then can we fully eliminate the so-called impedance mismatch, making it possible to express all our business logic in terms of the persistent data model, with the least amount of friction. So, the million-dollar question is what should that fusion look like? And, as mentioned before, in particular, we have to consider how to deal with relationships.

Suppose we have the following simple data model with two entities and a relationship (Figure 6-1).

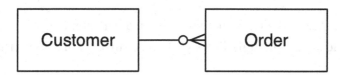

***Figure 6-1.*** *Sample model 1*

---

**Note**    As in the rest of this book, I'm using a simplified crow's foot notation here,[1] in which a straight line means singular cardinality, a crow's foot means plural cardinality, and a circle means that side of the relationship is optional.

---

In this model, a Customer may have placed zero, one, or multiple orders, and an Order is always associated with a single Customer. Suppose a Customer has two attributes, called name and id. To refer to these attributes, it generally suffices to refer to the name of the attribute, like so, in SQL:

```
SELECT NAME FROM CUSTOMER WHERE ID = 123
```

---

[1]James Martin and Clive Finkelstein, *Information Engineering* (Carnforth, England: Savant Institute, 1981).

In the case of an object database, you write something like this in the programming language at hand:

```
Customer customer
    = database.singleObjectQuery("Customer where id = 123");
customer.getName();
```

Accessing an attribute like name can easily be translated to a persistence-aware programming language, for example, with a syntax such as this:

```
customer.name
```

or

```
customer name
```

in which customer is a variable that refers to a persistent entity Customer. I will use the latter Smalltalk-like style (spaces instead of dots) throughout this book.

It gets more complicated if we incorporate relationships in a query. Suppose we want to know on which dates the Customer "Company X" has placed orders.

If we are dealing with an object database in combination with an object-oriented third-generation programming language (3GL), the code may look like this:

```
Customer customerX = database.singleObjectQuery(
    "Customer where name = 'Company X'");
List<Order> orders = customerX.getOrders();
foreach (Order order in orders) {
    ... order.getDate() ...
};
```

In the case of SQL, we would write

```
SELECT O.DATE FROM CUSTOMER C
JOIN ORDER O ON O.CUSTOMER_ID = C.ID
WHERE C.NAME = 'Company X'
```

And in the case of Cypher (Neo4j, a graph database),

```
MATCH (customer:Customer{name:"Company X"})
   -[:HAS_PLACED]->(orders)
RETURN orders
```

What the examples highlight is that every database architecture has a completely different perspective on relationships. In an object database, we see a relationship from Customer to Order as a list object that contains references to Orders. The Order class will probably have methods to set and get the Customer related to that Order. This then represents the one (1) side of the one-to-many (1:N) relationship, which we're expected to keep in sync with the list that represents the many (N) side. In SQL, it already looks completely different, as in the relational model, we can only represent relationships by the use of a foreign key. In the Cypher example, we see how in a graph database you refer to a relationship by utilizing its name, HAS_PLACED in this case.

All these variants have their drawbacks. In an object database, you traverse through relationships by explicitly iterating through the lists that represent them. That is exactly what to expect in the realm of an object-oriented programming language, but it makes it impossible to combine this with a query optimizer, as in SQL, to automatically figure out more efficient access paths. Some object databases come with their own query language, in which you can filter objects, as in the singleObjectQuery() example. But we ignore that for now, as their purpose is typically just to find an initial object or set of objects. All other data access is done by means of navigating from object to object. Suppose an Order has further details in an entity called OrderLine, and we want to count how many products were ordered. This might look as follows:

```
int totalNumberOfProducts = 0;
List<Order> orders = customerX.getOrders();
foreach (Order order in orders) {
    List<OrderLine> orderLines = order.getLines();
    foreach (OrderLine line in orderLines) {
        totalNumberOfProducts += line.getCount();
    }
    ...
}
```

As stated, because a large proportion of the query execution happens within the 3GL, the options for a database engine to optimize this type of navigational querying are very limited. It is typically a combination of smart caching and hints you can give to the database to prevent too much network round-trips.

In this sense, you're far better off with SQL.

```
SELECT SUM(OL.COUNT) FROM ORDER_LINES OL
JOIN ORDERS O ON O.ID = OL.ORDER_ID
JOIN CUSTOMER C ON C.ID = O.CUSTOMER_ID
WHERE C.NAME = 'Company X'
```

By definition, an SQL query is fully executed on the database server. A single round-trip suffices to get the answer. But above all, it offers possibilities for the database engine to find the most efficient way to execute the query, for example, in this case, by first only working out the order-ids, then using an index to find the matching order lines and adding the counts in one fell swoop.

The readability, however, did not really improve with this SQL example. In the object database example, we can at least clearly see that we retrieve the Orders of a Customer, and then the OrderLine instances per Order. In SQL, this translates into references to the foreign keys ORDER_ID and CUSTOMER_ID. And a foreign key, by definition, always references from the many to the one side of the relationship. As a consequence, you can never write something like "Given Customer X, give me all its Orders." You always have to reverse the way you think about such a request. It gets even more difficult if it is not clear to the reader which foreign key goes with what relationship, let alone if you are dealing with a compound key (two or more attributes together being the key). To summarize, SQL is well-equipped to deal with relationships, but it is not very expressive when it comes to referring to them. This can really undermine the readability of more complex queries and, for that reason, makes it very hard to judge a query's correctness, even for experts.

In a graph database, relationships have a clear name, often in the form of a verb or phrase, such as HAS_PLACED, in the preceding example. But in Neo4j (in which the example is written), you can only name the relationship in one direction. As in SQL, this means that you may have to refer to the relationship in the opposite direction from which you have to navigate it. To do so, you reverse the arrow -[ ]-> into <-[ ]-. So, to determine the Customer to which an Order belongs, you write

```
MATCH (order:Order{id:456})
    <-[:HAS_PLACED]- (customer)
RETURN customer
```

Again, this does not exactly contribute to readability. Of course, for such a simple query, this is not a big deal, but it is a whole different ball game if you involve multiple relationships in a more complex query.

# Relationships or Properties?

Simplifying the traversal of relationships in queries has several advantages. It will certainly contribute to the readability of queries, and, as said, this in turn helps in determining the correctness of a query. But as you will see, it can especially be beneficial when trying to fuse queries into a general-purpose programming language.

Fortunately, we don't have to look far and wide for a solution. Let's take a sample query and delve a little deeper into what a relationship actually is, and how we can refer to it from within a query.

Suppose we extend the earlier model, by including a relationship between OrderLine and an entity called Product (see Figure 6-2).

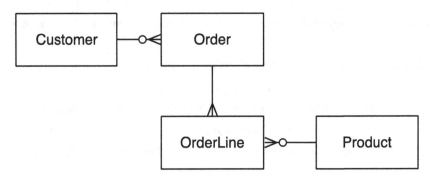

***Figure 6-2.*** *Sample model 2*

And suppose we want to ask the following question: How many times did the company with id "123" order product "X"? Translated to SQL, this might look like the following:

```
SELECT COUNT(*) FROM ORDER_LINE OL
JOIN PRODUCT P ON P.ID = OL.PRODUCT_ID
JOIN ORDER O ON O.ID = OL.ORDER_ID
WHERE P.NAME = 'X'
AND O.CUSTOMER_ID = 123
```

What immediately becomes obvious is that many more words are needed to formulate this query in SQL, as opposed to in plain English. Even if we remove potential ambiguity by using parentheses and the exact (sort of) entity names, the textual version still remains shorter.

```
number of times (order-lines with product 'X' of orders of
(customer with id 123))
```

Of course, no one relishes interpreting queries in natural language within the context of a formal programming language. But we can certainly define a formal language that, on the one hand, aligns with the way we would naturally formulate in English and, on the other, is unambiguous and strict enough to operate as expressions within the context of a programming language. Just as in mathematics, such a formal notation might even be more compact than the natural language counterpart.

The reason why the natural language version is shorter is because we use the construct "A of B," such as, for example "orders of customer," to refer to related entities. Nothing groundbreaking, but it is exactly what we need. What it comes down to is that we may consider a relationship as a role that two related entities have toward each other. Such a role virtually always can be written as a noun, often simply being the name of the other entity, in both directions.

There are schools, such as semantic data modeling and variations of ER modeling (e.g., UML's Logical Data Modeling, see Figure 6-3), that prefer naming relationships using a verb or a phrase.

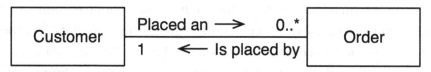

**Figure 6-3.** *An example of UML LDM naming both directions of a relationship*

You've seen this concept being used in the earlier Neo4j examples, in which the relationship between Customer and Order is given the name HAS_PLACED.

Language-wise this seems convenient, because it allows you to write something that closely resembles a sentence, such as "Customer X has placed Order Y." But this is mostly from the perspective of a predicate in the sense of a true/false statement. Instead, if we regard a relationship as two intertwined inverse roles, it is easy to see how we can suffice with a noun instead of a verb. It is what we humans use to describe the world, most of the time. For example, we simply say "table legs," rather than "legs that support the table," and "paint color," instead of "color that gives tint to the paint." This is because when we associate things with one another, what we intend to say is usually clear from the context. Often, the name of the other entity fits the bill. If it doesn't, for example, because there are multiple relationships between the same entities, we can pick an alternative noun, indicating the specific roles they have in these relationships.

Another interesting thing is that, at least in English, "A of B" means the same as "B A," just as "legs of a table" indicates the same relationship as "table legs" and "color of paint" is the same as "paint color." The latter is not only briefer; it is also more useful for so-called *property chaining*, which I will introduce in the next section.

So, to conclude, we can simply say

```
customer orders
```

to refer to the orders of a customer.

Of course, this is not entirely different than what is done in some programming languages and expression languages. In tools that allow you to query a hierarchical data structure, such as JSON, XML, or a DOM-tree, you may be allowed to say something like `customer.orders` (jQuery) or `customer/orders` (XPATH). And there is even some resemblance to what you would do in an object-oriented language: `customers.getOrders()`, except for the fact that `getOrders()` is an explicit method invocation, and we are looking for a more conceptual form that's not tied to any particular implementation. If your query says `customer orders` somewhere, that should purely mean that you are referring to the specific relationship between customers and orders. It should not imply that a method is invoked with the name orders. Neither should it assume the presence of an array or list containing these orders. That is something we can better leave to the compiler and the (database) runtime. Perhaps the phrase `customer orders` is part of a larger query, and the query optimizer is able to conclude that, within the current context, it suffices to just count the number of orders, without actually retrieving them, or perhaps solely to determine if there is at least one instance, such as with an SQL `EXISTS`.

If we view relationships in this light, we can sort of consider them properties, just like attributes, at least in the sense of how we refer to them from within a query, because, on the other hand, there are, of course, fundamental differences with regular attributes. Let's look into that further.

First of all, relationships are nearly always bidirectional, an aspect that does not apply to attributes. This means that when defining a relationship from entity A to entity B, you might also have to indicate what that relationship is called from the perspective of entity B. Only then can you state both

```
customer orders
```

and

```
order customer      // customer that placed the order
```

`customer`, in this example, is the inverse property of `orders`. However, and this is essential, we shouldn't view this as two separate properties being kept in sync. We are dealing with a single relationship for which you just use a different name, depending on your current perspective. The act of adding an Order to a Customer implies that the Order is becoming associated with that same Customer, and vice versa. With this conceptual way of thinking, we can leave all the technical details to implement the relationships concerned (e.g., foreign keys, lists, hash maps, or others) to the database engine itself. Whether this is still configurable or handled fully automatic is not relevant. It is the separation that matters here.

The strict distinction of a conceptual perspective on both data and queries, as opposed to a technical implementation of those elements, is what was proposed in the ANSI-SPARC architecture in 1975.[2] (See Figure 6-4.)

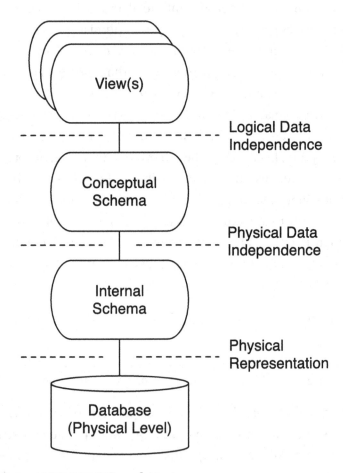

*Figure 6-4.* *ANSI-SPARC architecture*

---

[2]ANSI Study Group on Database Management Systems, *Interim Report*, 7, no. 2, Association for Computing Machinery, 1975.

One of the foundations of this architecture is that the conceptual level does not make any statements regarding the physical representation, as this is reserved for the internal schema. The same principle was written down by the inventor of the relational theory, Edgar F. Codd, as the 8th rule in his 12-rule manifesto,[3] called "Physical data independence." It was never implemented rigidly, but SQL comes a long way. This is why you only have to indicate *what* you want and not *how* to get it, the idea being that you can change the internal storage without disrupting the table definitions. This is, of course, not true in every respect, but the fact that you can move around with tables spaces, indexes, and other technicalities without changing your queries is still a reflection of Codd's rule number 8.

In theory, all relationships are bidirectional, in the sense that a relationship can always be viewed as a set of two properties that are each other's inverse, but exceptions can apply. For example, when referencing to data in external systems. Suppose that from an order system you specify a relationship with customers in a separate customer system you do not own. It would be odd if the owner of the customer system suddenly sees an inverse property appear in his data model. Conceptually, however, this is still a bidirectional relationship. Within the context of the order system, it might still be possible to ask for the orders of a customer, despite the customer system being oblivious to this.

Another attribute of relationships is that you have to specify the cardinality and optionality for both sides of the relationship, singular or plural, and optional or mandatory. In some modeling techniques, this is indicated by a minimum (0 or 1) and a maximum (1 or N) for both sides of the relationship. By their very nature, many relationships are one-to-many. But one-to-one relationships can certainly exist, in which case, one side is often optional. A strong case can also be made for many-to-many

---

[3]E. F. Codd, "An Evaluation Scheme for Database Management Systems That Are Claimed to Be Relational," *Proceedings of the Second International Conference on Data Engineering* (Washington, DC: IEEE Computer Society, 1986), pp. 720–729.

relationships. Most database architectures only support these indirectly, for example, by defining an additional linking table yourself. But they occur in many real-world models, and especially from the perspective of querying, it is good to give them full support. Let's consider the model in Figure 6-5.

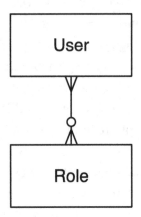

***Figure 6-5.*** *Users with roles*

If we are interested in the roles of a user, we should not have to write

```
user user-roles roles
// user-roles being an linking table
```

but just

```
user roles
```

There are data modeling methodologies in which relationships can themselves have attributes, referred to as so-called associative entities. It remains to be seen, however, whether it is necessary to support this explicitly. In the end, it is a matter of perspective. We may view such an associative entity as just another entity. And if we must add such an attribute later to what initially was a pure relationship, we can treat this as a refactoring of the data model.

Finally, we have to consider the naming of relationships. There is often no reason to name a relationship differently from the entity it refers to, and vice versa for the opposite side. But, as said before, there may be cases in which this is not a feasible rule, as in the model in Figure 6-6.

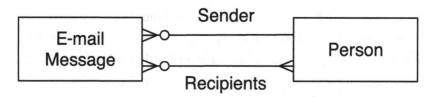

***Figure 6-6.*** *Multiple roles between two entities*

Both sender and recipients of an E-mail Message are Persons, but they can serve two different roles—that of sender or recipient. The solution is as easy as to make an exception to the rule and name both relationships differently, so we can write:

```
email-message sender
```

and

```
email-message recipients
```

To summarize, relationships really are a thing of their own, but naming them according to the roles they represent makes them as easy to refer to within a query as plain attributes.

But wait, we're not there yet.

# Property Chaining

Purely with the fact that we can refer to relationships as being properties, we still don't have a fully-fledged query language. The power of this principle will, however, become apparent with something that closely mimics natural language, something we will call *property chaining.*

Property chaining is similar to so-called method chaining, but it uses conceptual properties rather than methods calls. An example of a method chain in a programming language is something like this:

```
orderLine.getOrder().getCustomer().getName()
```

This allows us to find the name of the Customer that corresponds to the OrderLine at hand. However, every step in a method chain consists of an actual method call. And for that reason, it is bound to a specific implementation. We can start calling it property chaining when we translate this to a much more conceptual form:

```
order-line order customer name
```

With `order` we get the associated order, and then `customer` provides us with the customer. The final step is retrieving the customer's name.

Using the same principle, we can also write very different queries, such as:

```
customer-x orders order-lines products names
```

We can interpret this as: "all names of products that were ever ordered by customer-x." This example is interesting, because it goes beyond what is possible in a 3GL method chain. Imagine, we wrote this:

```
customerX.getOrders().getOrderLines()
    .getProducts().getNames()
```

This runs aground already at `getOrderLines()`, because the object that `getOrders()` returns will probably be an instance of a collection class. Even when the language in question returns a type-safe list utilizing generics, it is still not possible to invoke a method like `getOrderLines()` on it. A class `List<Order>` may very well be associated with the class type `Order`, but other than that, it still remains a generic List object.

By allowing a construct like this:

```
customer-x orders order-lines
```

we created the foundation for a set-oriented language. And with that, we can have a rule that says the following: if within the context of a set of objects (customer-x orders) we refer to a property (order-lines) of the individual objects in that set, then the result is a new set of all the related objects. Following this rule, the preceding expression will return all order-lines of all orders of customer-x.

Property chaining is certainly not a totally new phenomenon. There are many query and template languages in which you can specify a path in similar ways, such as with this XPATH expression:

```
customerX/order/orderLine
```

Yet, this type of path expression is typically in terms of a hierarchical structure you are querying, and a data model in a database is not necessarily purely hierarchical. The query

```
customer-x orders order-lines
```

expresses the traversal of two one-to-many relationships that together form a hierarchy. If, however, we extend the query by getting the related products, like so,

```
customer-x orders order-lines products
```

the query ends with the traversal of a one-to-many relationship in the reverse direction: from many to one. That's because products will be in a separate table (or whatever form) and just be referenced from the order lines.

With hierarchical structures such as XML or JSON, this is not a logical construct. That is because a hierarchy, by definition, cannot contain a many-to-one relationship in this reverse direction. If a hierarchy would contain the product details, it has to be either a duplicate of products per order line or substituted with a reference (foreign key). So, it would be either a data redundancy or technically changing the way we access the relationship.

In a database, this limitation does not exist, because we model data as we see fit: as a network of entities.

In a functional or modern object-oriented language supporting map() operations, we might write the preceding query as something like this:

```
customerX.getOrders()
    .map({order | order.getOrderLines()})
    .map({orderLine | orderLine.getProduct()})
```

Unfortunately, given the ultimate goal of conceiving a conceptual query language, the use of explicit calls to a map() function, in a way, is just a workaround for the fact that we can't express ourselves in terms of sets in these languages. As stated before, the only way to transcend this limitation is to extend the idea of object orientation into set orientation.

An interesting question is what must happen if a *product* has been ordered multiple times. If that is the case, a standard map() operation will return a list containing duplicates. Does this have actual meaning in practice, or does de-duplicating the result make more sense?

If, in a conversation with another human, you ask which products a certain customer has ordered, you don't expect the answer to be something like:

Product A

Product B

Product B

Product C

Product B

as, of course, the expected answer to that question is:

>  Product A

>  Product B

>  Product C

You could argue that you always have to explicitly enforce this de-duplication yourself. For example, like so:

```
customer-x orders order-lines products deduplicate
```

This is kind of what you would do with a DISTINCT in SQL. However, as you will see in later examples, it is a much more logical choice to make this happen automatically. This might take some getting used to for some people, because we're so accustomed to the fact that a list may refer to the same object multiple times.

Conceptually it is actually better to think in terms of sets than sticking with the idea of a list. It is for this reason that I am talking about a *set-oriented* programming language here.

Realize, too, that physical de-duplication is only required in certain situations. Duplicates can only occur when you traverse a many-to-one relationship in the *one* direction, as with the *product* reference in the example above. Even then, action is only required if it would otherwise have consequences for the end result or purpose of a query. For example, if you only want to know if a certain object exists in a given set, de-duplication makes no sense. And if you traverse a whole chain of relationships, it might be more efficient to de-duplicate only at the end of that chain. Both are perfect examples of decisions to leave up to a query optimizer.

Then, there is a feature I snuck into the earlier examples but didn't address so far. It's about the use of singular vs. plural names for the elements in a query. If we strictly used the names of the relationships, our example would look like this:

```
customer-x orders order-lines product
```

That's because each `order-line` is linked to a single `product`. However, owing to property chaining, the result is a set of products. In plain English, we would never say

*product* sold to customer-x (not a typo)

which is why the following also makes more sense:

`customer-x orders order-lines products`

With this, we make it explicit that we expect multiple products to be returned. It certainly makes queries much more readable. We can accomplish this feature by specifying both the singular and plural names for each element in the data model. This may sound a bit far-fetched, but it is kind of the set-oriented variant of what we already do in object-oriented languages with something like this:

```
Product            // a single product
List<Product>      // a list of products
```

And it is not just about using a plural name instead of writing `List<>`. It is much more conceptual, because we leave it to the compiler plus runtime to work out the exact implementation. So, we defer dealing with sets to the language itself. But more important, it also reflects the fact that we talk about a set of a certain type. `List<Product>` is a technical construct in an object-oriented language associated with a `Product` class, but it still remains a generic collection class by itself. In a set-oriented programming language, we can use the plural form to really represent a set of a certain type. And we can make the plural form applicable to attributes, too, which allows us to write something like this:

`customer-x orders order-lines products names`

This results in the names of the products, instead of references to products.

To prevent being forced to specify a plural name for every attribute in a model, we could have a special symbol to indicate plurality, say, with an asterisk, so you can write name* instead of names. And the integrated development environment could automatically refactor this, if we specify a plural name at a later moment. On the other hand, it is probably not that much work to do all this upfront.

The idea of using both singular and plural names in a programming language is not a totally new one. Have a look at AppleScript, if you want to see examples. We could see it as a form of type-safety on the level of sets. It does not only help us to know that the object type is correct, it can also make sure that the cardinality of an expression is what you expect.

Take this expression, in which we apply a filter predicate (id = 123, more on filters in the next section):

```
customers [ id = 123 ] names
```

Suppose we specify customer id in the data model to be unique across all customers. In that case, we might much rather write this:

```
customers [ id = 123 ] name
```

or, even better,

```
customer [ id = 123 ] name
```

Such an expression is both type-safe and, let's give it a name, cardinality-safe. It is also very readable, because it closely resembles natural language while still being a formal language. No one will ask for the "names of the customers with id 123" if you very well know there can be only one with that id.

As stated before, some elements of property chaining can be found in existing products; however, the form, as described previously, takes it a step further. It's not limited to querying hierarchical structures. Instead, it can describe any arbitrary path in every imaginable data model. It is purely conceptual, in the sense that it is disparted from any technical

107

implementation details. And, in addition to type-safety, it delivers cardinality-safety. So, it's a solid basis for a set-oriented programming language that I will elaborate on in a later chapter.

# Filters

It's time now for another essential element of any query language: filters (*where-clauses* or *predicates*, depending on your perspective). A where-clause is perhaps even the first thing that comes to mind when you think of queries. It is not where the biggest challenges lie. Because that, as shown in the previous section, is mostly in the way we model relationships and how we can refer to them using property chaining. But if we combine property chaining with filters, a powerful combination emerges: nicely compact expressions that are very good candidates to be integrated into a fully-fledged programming language.

Let's start with some syntax. In this book, I have chosen square brackets to represent filters, in line with many template languages, such as XPATH, as in this example:

```
products [ name = 'Bicycle' ]
```

What type of brackets to use is obviously a matter of taste, but, still, this bracket form is itself more universal than something such as WHERE. A so-called where-clause is an artifact of SQL, and it does not go along with property chaining very well. Suppose we want to know which orders totaling more than 10,000 were placed in region 4. Then this:

```
customers [ region = 4 ] orders [ amount > 10000 ]
```

fits better with the concept of property chaining than this:

```
(customers where region = 4) orders where amount  >  10000
```

The square brackets naturally indicate the boundaries of the logical expressions and, therefore, do not interfere with the property chaining itself.

You could also question why we would require a special operator for filtering at all. Most modern programming languages support closures that can be input for a `filter()` function to write something like this:

```
customers filter({ c | c.region = 4 })
   orders filter({ o | o.amount > 10000 })
```

However, for building persistence-aware queries, this is exactly what we don't want. First, as with `map()`, it implies a certain way of execution. What we need instead is a query optimizer able to analyze the query as an abstract syntax tree (AST) and then optimize it. We could have a compiler recognize the filter({...}) syntax and handle it as you would have with square brackets, but it makes a lot more sense for first-class citizens, being a filter construct in this case, to be made to look like first-class citizens.

Second, closures are a kind of anonymous functions. That's why you might need to specify parameters, such as the `c` and `o` in the example. Granted, some languages introduced tricks to shorten the syntax (such as *$0* in Swift), and in dynamic and functional languages, it's even a whole other story. But if you think about it, there is actually no need for parameters in a filter. This is because the logical expression in a filter is always going to be in terms of the types of objects being filtered. This means that in a query such as the following:

```
customers [ logic expression ]
```

the logical default is to refer to properties of a customer, just as you can directly refer to a property of an object within a method of such an object. It is a matter of scope. Later, I will go into the details of this concept, which I will call a subcontext. This will also explain how we can still refer to the outer scope of such a filter. But for now, it is enough to conclude that we can make do with just two brackets and still have a type-safe and cardinality-safe filter expression.

Obviously, we will require a set of basic operators, such as and, or, >, etc., the usual suspects. But, in addition to this, many queries also require aggregation functions, such as count() or sum(). Interestingly, we can fit those within the idea of property chaining, by introducing so-called *set-level functions* (or *set functions*) to write something like this:

```
customers count
```

This will tell us how many customers we have. And

```
orders amounts sum
```

returns the total amount of all orders. A set function is a function that is associated with a specific type of object, but instead of applying to individual objects, it operates on a set of those objects. For count(), this is not so different than in an object-oriented language, but it becomes interesting with a function such as sum(). By defining sum() as a set function for number objects, it can do number-specific things. This is another benefit of this book's proposed set orientation, in which sets are not represented by generic instances of collection classes but instead by an integral concept within the language itself.

Let's combine in a few examples the things you've learned so far.

*"All customers who ever ordered product X"*

```
customers [ orders
    order-lines [ product name = 'X' ] count > 0 ]
```

*"All customers in region 4 who never ordered more than one product per order"*

```
customers [ region = 4
    and orders [ order-lines count > 1 ] count = 0 ]
```

*"The total turnover on products that were sold at least 100 times"*

```
products [ order-lines count >= 100 ]
    order-lines orders amounts sum
```

110

These examples are limited to what we have discussed so far, but the possibilities are endless. The essential thing to take away here is that filtering in this way is a natural fit with the concept of property chaining. So, we end up with two building blocks that combine in any desirable fashion.

# Summary

In this chapter, I have introduced a few concepts that will eventually lead us to a unified conceptual data model and an accompanying programming language. Because the essence of persistent data is querying that data, we started at that end of the equation.

You have learned that with most database architectures, traversing relationships is somewhat cumbersome. The use of collection classes to represent relationships in the case of object databases (but also with ORM tools, etc.) leaves no room for far-reaching optimizations. In SQL, the concept of foreign keys hampers readability, and in a graph database, there is a lot of emphasis on the name of the relationship, while the name of the other entity often suffices to refer to that relationship.

Modeling a relationship as a bidirectional property allows us to stay very close to the structure and compactness of natural language. Having such a direct way to refer to relationships enables us to make them more explicit and conceptual at the same time. The conceptual aspect decouples the query language from any specific implementation, making it possible to write *what* we are looking for, rather than *how* we want the query to be executed, just as in SQL, but with the advantages of an object or entity model.

By specifying both a singular and a plural name for relationships (and data model elements in general), queries become more readable and, as a result, easier to validate. This means that in addition to type-safety, we can now strive for cardinality-safety, with all the advantages this brings when it comes to code completion, refactoring, and so-called schema evolution.

Finally, you have seen how we can apply the concept of property chaining to refer to every possible path in a data model. We adapted it to make meaningful use of cardinality-safety, discussed the case for implicit de-duplication, and added the idea of filters.

With the combination of property chaining and filtering, we have defined the foundation for a set-oriented programming language. In the next chapter, I will talk about data manipulation and how all these concepts together lead us in the direction of a unified conceptual data model.

# CHAPTER 7

# The IR Model

*You can have data without information, but you cannot have
information without data.*

—Daniel Keys Moran

In the previous chapter, you have seen that changing the way we write
queries cannot be separate from the structure of the underlying meta
model. This is because the way we model relationships has a direct impact
on how we can refer to those relationships in a query.

But this interaction does not only apply to data retrieval. With
regard to the creation, modification, and deletion of objects (records),
we also have to consider both the integration into the language and the
consequences of the way we model data. We may view instances of entities
as objects, deliberately blurring the boundaries between these terms. In
programming languages, objects are generally created with a new or similar
statement, after which you attach them to other existing objects, using
a setter, or by adding them to a collection. Garbage collection can then
subsequently dispose objects that are no longer necessary. This is also how
object databases typically integrate with object-oriented programming
languages. However, this strategy has its disadvantages. In this chapter, you
will see in what sense and will I propose an alternative that better fits the
unified and conceptual data model that we strive for here.

Deleting objects sounds like a relatively simple topic. Unfortunately,
deletion in the context of an application and, therefore, in the context of a
database, is not always as straightforward as you might think. For example,

© Jos Jong 2019
J. Jong, *Vertically Integrated Architectures*,
https://doi.org/10.1007/978-1-4842-4252-0_7

what should happen to objects that refer to the object to be deleted? And what if we want to maintain a history in the database with the purpose of auditing, or to implement undo/redo features? Maybe it is better to speak of archiving rather than deletion.

In addition to the creation and removal of objects, this chapter will also pay attention to the manipulation of relationships and modifying attributes, not only for operations on single objects, but also on sets of objects. The update operations I will introduce shortly, together with the query expressions from the previous chapter, are the foundations for a persistence-aware programming language. A language that is

- Object-oriented, in the sense that it sees entities as objects with properties and methods

- Set-oriented, in the sense that sets of objects are first-class citizens

- Functional, in the sense that every expression and function is purely functional

- Imperative, in the sense that updates, despite the functional aspect, are allowed, but only in procedures earmarked as such

## Unifying Ownership

One of the main propositions in this book is the tight integration of database access within a programming language. In the previous chapter, you've seen how the way we model data is directly interlinked with the way we query that same data. The same is true for the way we create, modify, and delete data.

Let's first see how we can embed the creation and deletion of persistent objects in a programming language (we'll look at attributes and relationships later on). With that, we have to deal with such things as ownership, composition, access paths, and cascading deletes. Existing database architectures all have their own specific approach in this regard. But we will see that we can combine all these aspects into a single unified concept that for this reason also further contributes to the integration of update statements within the programming language.

As you have seen in the previous chapter, we can view instances of entities as objects. Therefore, it seems obvious to create persistent objects in the same manner as we do in-memory objects. This is precisely the strategy followed by object databases. The creation of a persistent object in an object database may look like this:

```
Project project = new Project();
project.setName("Project X");
databaseRoot.getAllProjects().add(project);
```

Object databases employ different approaches to determine that Project is intended to be a persisted object, sometimes by inheriting from a special PersistentObject class, sometimes by way of a special new operator, or indirectly by the assignment to another persistent object, such as in the preceding example, in which the project is added to a list of all projects in the database.

Even if such an add() operation is not required to mark an object as persistent, you still need a way to provide access to all objects in the database. Object databases are, therefore, often represented by a root object or a root dictionary, with every object in the database directly or indirectly reachable via that root, to make them accessible. A persistent garbage collector may use the fact that an object is no longer reachable via such a root as a reason to delete it.

An interesting question now is whether we really need such root access paths, and why something like new Project is not sufficient. After all, in SQL we can just write

```
INSERT INTO PROJECT(NAME) VALUES ('Project X');
```

While in the context of an object-oriented programming language, there is a difference between the creation of an object (new Project) and making it accessible by any means, this is not the case with SQL. In SQL, it is sufficient to define a table with the name PROJECT, and you don't have to specify what kind of records you want to add to that table, as this is apparent from the definition of the table itself.

There are two things at play here:

- The fact that in SQL, you do not need to add records to a database root

- The fact that in SQL, every record in a table has the exact same structure

The first has to do with the fact that every table, in a way, is a root table itself. That's because, within the context of a schema at least, all tables have a global scope. So, adding a record to a table immediately makes it accessible for queries. In object-oriented languages, something such as globally accessible lists of all objects never existed. That's why it made no sense to implement something like that with object databases.

The second has to do with polymorphism, or lack thereof in SQL. Imagine we have two kinds of projects: internal and external. In object-oriented databases, we can represent this with subclasses, so we can write something like this:

```
Project project = new ExternalProject();
projects.add(project);
```

The variable project and the list named projects are polymorphs, in the sense that they can contain either ExternalProject or InternalProject instances. The fact that the type of an object can differ from what you assign it to (a variable, list, or otherwise) is another reason why creation and assignment are separate, while this distinction does not exist in SQL. The question, however, is why we have to deal with this separation, even though we only need polymorphism once in a while. It makes sense to declare the most common case the default and only allow polymorphism by exception. In the next section, you will see how this simplifies the creation of object.

But it gets even simpler with a broader definition of something that is commonly called *composition*. A composition, in terms of an entity model, means that the life cycle of one entity is bound to that of another entity. For example, say we have a model with Projects containing Tasks. If a Task may never exist without a corresponding Project, then we speak of a composition. From this automatically follows that if a Project is deleted, all corresponding Tasks are deleted as well (or archived, but that's a later subject).

Let's further explore this example with Projects and project Tasks. The creation of a new Task in an object database could look as follows:

```
Task task = new Task();
task.name = "Task 1";
project.addTask(task);
```

In SQL, you would write

```
INSERT INTO TASK (PROJECT_ID, NAME) VALUES (123, 'Task 1');
```

and in a JSON document database, you would do something like this (assuming we update a document with all projects in memory using JavaScript):

```
project.tasks.push(
    {
        "name": "Task 1"
    }
);
```

We see how, in an object database, it can be sufficient to add a Task to a Project. Adding them to a root collection is not needed, because we can access them via the projects, as long as projects themselves are accessible in any way. With JSON, we see something similar: the first object in a JSON document is, kind of, the local root for that document. Everything else is accessible via the hierarchy below. In contrast to all this, with SQL, you access all records via their respective table name.

Composition is about ownership, in the sense that removing an object removes all underlying objects. In a JSON document, this happens implicitly. In SQL, you can accomplish this by specifying cascading delete rules. In an object database, a garbage collector can take care of this.

The interesting thing now is that ownership does not only happen between objects. In a way, a table is owner of all its records, and in an object database, a root index is owner of all objects accessible via that root. Ownership is everywhere. Every level in a database, even a database schema, a table, a root index, or a whole JSON document can be seen as part of one big composition that together forms the database as a whole.

This may seem a bit far-fetched, but if we view the whole database as one big composition with sublevels of ownership, we can actually merge such things as ownership, schemas, compositions, and cascading deletes into a single unified concept. In the next section, you will see how.

# The IR Model

The model that follows from this unification of ownership is what we will call the *IR*, or *item-relationship,* model from now on. There is, of course, nothing wrong with the term *entity* or the ER model that the IR model is based on, but the term *item* is more suitable for a variety of reasons.

The word *item* works well when we want to refer to so-called *subitems.* The significance of this will become apparent shortly. Besides this, the word *entity* is more often used to mean "entity type," rather than referring to a single record. But *item* also bridges the terminologies of databases and programming languages. *Item* is a nice, generic English word for *something* in a list. It is also a suitable alternative to the word *record*, which has a somewhat technical connotation, and we stay away from the word *object*, which we then can retain as a generic super-type of both items and values (I'll return to that later).

The following encompass the IR model:

- Every database is represented by a single root item.

- Every other item is directly or indirectly a subitem of that root.

What do we accomplish with this? First, we are able to model compositions such as

```
projects
    tasks
        subtasks
```

in which tasks are subitems of projects, and subtasks are in turn subitems of tasks. But because the database itself is an item, the overall structure looks as follows:

```
database             // the root item, a singleton
    projects
        tasks
            subtasks
```

Every item type whose life cycle does not depend on that of another item can be defined as a subitem of the database, as with both orders and products in this example:

```
database
    orders
        order-lines
    products
```

To make sure that an order-line can refer to a product, we use a regular relationship.

```
database
    orders
        order-lines
            product -> database product
    products
        order-lines -> database orders order-lines
```

---

**Note**    This notation is not intended to be a formal grammar. It is just a way to write down the examples here.

---

In the IR model, we distinguish between two types of relationships:

- Relationships that imply ownership, exclusively being the relationships between items and their subitems

- All other relationships. These are not about ownership and, therefore, by definition, cross the subitem hierarchy. I will call these *associations* (in the sense of a subcategory of relationships).

The basic premise behind this idea is that although a data model is not necessarily hierarchical, ownership always is. If ownership weren't hierarchical, it would mean that an item can have multiple owners. Then the question of when it should be deleted would arise. True, multiple owners can be useful in some models; it is just not very common. When we really need it, nothing stops us from defining the item and taking control of its deletion using delete triggers or something similar.

A hierarchy has always been a good start for a data model. It was the basis for hierarchical databases in the 1960s, and a JSON document is also a hierarchical structure. But, sadly, all those implementations offer little or no support for nonhierarchical relationships. In this sense, the IR model takes the hierarchy from hierarchical databases, supplementing it with nonhierarchical relationships (associations), as can be found in ER models.

Identifying some relationships in a model as *owning* and the rest as *not-owning* does not sound like a big deal. When drawing an ER or UML model, it is often nothing more than using another type of line or arrow. However, there is a lot of potential that goes with this distinction.

The first and most fundamental advantage has everything to do with what was discussed in the previous section. It makes it possible to no longer distinguish between the creation of an item and establishing the ownership relationship. This has everything to do with scope. The reason why in an SQL database we can create a record by simply referring to a table name is because it occurs within the scope of a schema. Items can be regarded as kinds of objects, and where in an object-oriented language every method is executed within the context of a certain object, we can apply the same principle when creating new items. Within the context of the database item, it could suffice to say

```
x = new project
```

This creates a new project item in the database and assigns it to the variable x. But similarly, within the context of a project, we can write

```
y = new task
```

and because this creation occurs within the context of a given project, the new task automatically becomes a subitem of that same project.

There are several ways to create a context. Within the body of a method, the so-called this (or self) object can be the context. But we may also create a temporary local context. Suppose variable order-x refers to an order. Then we may write

```
order-x:
    y = new order-line
```

The colon and the indentation here mean "within the context of," comparable to a with keyword in some existing programming languages (such as JavaScript, Pascal, and others), but with greater consequences.

We do not even have to assign new items to variables. Within the context of the database root item, we can just write

```
new project:
    name = 'Project X'
    new task:
        name = 'Task 1'
```

We can read this as "create a new project item within the database, give it the name Project X, and create a first task for this project with the name Task 1."

Because, in this way, all new operations occur within the scope of another item, and because the database itself is an item, there is no distinction between creating objects at root level and at sublevels. Instead of having to indicate the parent item with every item created, we can just do this within the context of that parent item. This can also be in methods associated with that parent item, so we can have item types that are self-contained, in the sense that they are not dependent on a global database schema. This is true for items on every level in the hierarchy.

Despite the fact that we regard some relationships as item/subitem relationships and the rest as associations, both are still relationships when we query them. So, we can still write

```
database projects tasks
```

By definition, an item/subitem relationship is always a bidirectional one. Suppose within the context of a task we want to access the name of the corresponding project, we can just write

```
project name
```

in which project refers to the parent of the task, being the project it belongs to.

122

An item/subitem relationship can only be one-to-many or one-to-one, and the parent can never be optional against its subitems. So, there is always exactly one `project` attached to a `task` via the item/subitem relationship. (There is no limit to what it is connected to via associations.) The default name for the inverse of an item/subitem relationship can be name of the parent type in question (`project`, in the preceding example), but we can override this, if required.

As stated, in this concept, the database is itself just a large composition. With this generic approach to ownership, new possibilities emerge at every level. We are able to define as many levels as we need. Suppose we first create a single project administration but later realize we want to distinguish between different administrations. We can then migrate the database to introduce a level in between, such as `administrations` in this example:

```
database
    administrations
        projects
            tasks
```

If we define `administrations` to be a one-to-many relationship, we can create multiple segregated `administrations`, each with its own `projects` and `tasks`. Even though these `projects` and `tasks` are separated from each other, they are still based on the same database schema, almost like a data model template.

We can also use this concept to have default behavior for copying items at any level in the database. Suppose we want to make a copy of the aforementioned Project X, we could then write

```
x = project [ name = 'Project X' ]
x copy:
    name = 'Project Y'
```

or, without involving a variable,

```
project [ name = 'Project X' ] copy:
    name = 'Project Y'
```

Such a copy, wherever it occurs in the hierarchy, will always be a so-called deep copy, as this follows from the definition of composition and ownership.

With this generic form of ownership, we have introduced something we know from file systems into the realm of databases. Within a file system, the root directory of a disk is also not different from any other subdirectory. By default, a copy of a directory is also a deep copy, unless, of course, symbolic links are detected, which have some resemblance to associations.

Despite this generic approach, the IR model is a completely schema-full model. Every item/subitem relationship you define is implicitly defining a unique item type, and every actual subitem you subsequently create will adhere to the rules (properties, constraints, etc.) of that type.

Because the IR model is explicit when it comes to ownership, there is no need for a garbage collector. Object-oriented languages require a garbage collector, because an object model does not articulate ownership. Because of this, an object may have multiple owners. By postulating a single-ownership hierarchy, the database can automatically perform cascading deletes and do without the overhead of a garbage collector. As said before, we may still be able to escape from this single ownership with something like delete triggers, but that would just be an exception to the rule.

Indirectly, the IR model has another advantage. Because of the absence of global scope, you are less likely to be hindered by naming conflicts. That is because the naming of an item/subitem relationship is a local affair within the concerning parent item. This is why we can have two item types named line, without running into trouble, as shown in the following example:

```
database
    orders
        lines
    invoices
        lines
```

In this model, `line` is something else within the context of an order, as opposed to within the context of an invoice. And from within the context of a database, we may write both:

```
orders lines
```

and

```
invoices lines
```

Owing to the absence of a global scope, every item type, in a way, is its own unit. Because of this, we probably have less or no need for such things as name qualifiers, modules, or packages (as with many programming languages). It also enables us to use more readable shortened names, like lines, and it could potentially encourage the reuse of parts of a model, as if they were separate modules.

To finish, let's think about the technical implications of the IR model. The fact that subitems can only be accessed via other items in the hierarchy does not mean that this must be reflected in the actual execution of a query. The IR model should be regarded as a purely conceptual model that leaves it up to the compiler and query engine to decide on the best access path. A query such as

```
invoices lines
```

does not mean the server has to traverse all the invoice records one at a time to determine the lines. And the query

```
invoices lines [ product name = 'X' ]
```

might be resolved by first consulting an index on product name and then using a foreign key index to find all the related lines. Regardless of whether the database itself decides which indexes are desired, or we have to define them ourselves, we have to view this separately from the conceptual model, just as in SQL and other database architectures.

Granted, most ideas incorporated in the IR model aren't totally new concepts. At its core, it is a hierarchical database model, based on the idea that ownership of data is nearly always hierarchical. Just like the ER model, it supports relationships in a way that allows us to refer to them in queries in an implementation-independent fashion. But from a different viewpoint, it is an object model, because item types can be seen as object classes, making it possible to define methods at the level of these item types. And while the IR model bears little resemblance to the relational model, it makes a strict distinction between how you write a query and the execution of that query, just like SQL.

The amalgamation of all these things delivers a lot.

- A new operation that, in contrast to object databases and object-relational mappers, does not separate the creation of persistent objects and the assignment of an access path to those objects

- Because of the local scope of new, there is less or no need to reference the global scope of a database.

- Because of this, you naturally get a subdivision of a larger model in submodels, which increases their potential for reuse.

- A conceptual model that does not hinge on to the underlying technical aspects and, therefore, gives the compiler and query optimizer more opportunities for optimization

- No need for a persistent garbage collector

- Implicit cascading-deletes behavior at every level of the model

- Deep-copy behavior comes out of the box.

- And, of course, the query capabilities, as discussed in the previous chapter

# Archiving Instead of Deleting

In theory, deleting an item is the inverse of creating an item. The extent to which this is true, however, strongly depends on what we actually mean by *delete*. In most information systems, we do not record the state of the world only as it is now but also what happened in the past. This introduces a temporal aspect to the concept of removing data. It means that deletion in many systems is better represented by an active=yes/no attribute than by actually wiping out a record. Let alone, there may be specific reasons to keep old records, for example, auditing requirements.

Let's look at this dilemma of physically deleting or not, using the earlier model with orders and products.

```
database (root)
    customers
        orders
            lines
                product -> product
                count
    products
        name
```

With new orders, you only want to be able to select a product that is still available for sale. So, if we no longer sell product X, it makes sense to delete it with a statement that could look like this:

```
delete product [ name = 'X' ]
```

---

**Note**    The idea here is that a delete statement removes all objects referenced by the expression that follows.

---

But suppose we made a sale with this product only yesterday. What happens then to order lines that refer to this product? In other words, what is the answer to this query within the context of such an order?

```
lines [ product name = 'X' ]
```

Even though product X is deleted, we probably still expect this query to return all order lines that pertain to product X. This, however, contradicts the fact that we don't want product X to be returned by this query:

```
database products
```

Another example is the following. Suppose we have not sold anything to a customer for a long time, and we'd rather hide the details of that customer when we search through the customers list. We could then opt to remove that customer. But we still might want to access the orders of that customer in the future. What it comes down to is that in many information systems, instead of physical deletion, in a lot of scenarios, we need something else.

Now let's look into something that is related. In many applications, it may be required or useful to know when a record was last modified, and some systems even go so far as to preserve previous values or keep track of who made the changes concerned. This could be owing to legal requirements, internal auditing rules, or just to make it easier to troubleshoot production disruptions.

It is certainly possible to address this with a custom design, such as using additional history tables or timestamp columns. However, this wheel is being reinvented time and time again, and there is actually a lot to be said to let the database take care of this itself. Apart from not having to build the logic to keep track of changes, it would also help when writing queries. In many situations, we want queries to return the *current* state of data, and it would help if the database engine, by default, filters out inactive records.

Then, concerning the tracking of changes, it is helpful to realize that databases, by their very nature, already record every modification into a journal or log file. They do this primarily to facilitate recovery, but it does not have to be limited to that purpose. Applications servers typically access a database with a single user account. If, instead, we make the database aware of the actual end user, it could also register who made each individual change. By subsequently making this information accessible via queries, we have a generic solution to a very common system requirement. As an application developer, you no longer have to invent this yourself; it will always be possible to travel back in time to see what happened; and it may even be useful for a handy undo/redo functionality toward the end user.

Keeping track of all historic changes in a database also shines a different light on the meaning of the term *delete*. It makes more sense to talk about *archiving* items instead of deleting them. As with many manual implementations, this mechanism could manifest itself with a Boolean archived attribute, but without the need to define that yourself. And by integrating this concept into the database and query language, we can take this a step further. We can make sure that instead of

```
products [ category = 4 and not archived ]
```

with the additional and not archived in every query, we can just write

```
products [ category = 4 ]
```

This could automatically exclude archived products. This makes sense as default behavior, when accessing items via the ownership path. So, if you ask for subitems via a query like this:

```
orders lines
```

it could, by default, be read as:

```
orders [ not archived ] lines [ not archived ]
```

When we traverse the data model using an association (a non-item/subitem relationship), it makes more sense to do the opposite: not filter out the archived items. For example, take this query:

```
order-x lines products
```

In most cases, we would probably want to interpret this as:

```
order-x lines [ not archived ] products
```

instead of

```
order-x lines [ not archived ] products [ not archived ]
```

That's because it makes no sense to hide archived products when showing order lines.

This automatic hiding or non-hiding of archived items could be default behavior, and we could still have a way to work around it, if we want to deviate from the general rule. For example, to get all orders, whether archived or not, we could have a special keyword that forces this to happen, such as the following:

```
orders [ archived-or-not ]
```

To conclude this section, we should also rethink cascading deletes. If items are archived instead of deleted, the whole idea of cascading deletes no longer has any meaning, but that's a matter of definition, of course. We can very well transform the concept of cascading deletes into cascaded archiving. This would mean that when you archive an item, all subitems of that item are implicitly archived too.

This book has no intention of going into all the details of these archiving and temporal aspects. That's up to an actual implementation or more research on this subject. The point of this section is just to show that temporal data and archiving data are so common that it makes a lot of sense to build them into the data model.

## Associations

In addition to the item/subitem relationships, the IR model also supports so-called associations. Both are relationships, but whereas item/subitem relationships determine an ownership hierarchy, associations cut across this hierarchy. We query them in the same way, but they are different in how we establish and break them.

With subitem relationships, the creation of an item cannot be viewed independent of the establishment of the relationship between the item and subitem. If order-x refers to an order, then this statement:

```
order-x:
    new line
```

creates a new order line as part of that order. In contrast, with an association, you always link two existing items to each other.

Let's look at a few examples. In this book, we will use the operator = for assignment and << for adding to a set. Suppose the variable order-line-x refers to an order line, then

```
order-line-x product =
    database product [ name = 'Product X' ]
```

associates the product with name 'Product X' with this order line. product from the perspective of an order line is a singular property. Thus, we can only associate one product at a time. If there already was an associated product, that existing association is removed, which, again implies clearing the referral from this product back to the order line. Although relationships can be viewed as two properties, they are actually an integrated always-in-sync concept.

The operator << is used to manipulate the plural side of a one-to-many or many-to-many association. If project-x refers to a project, then the following statement will add the person item referred to by person-x as a member:

```
project-x members << person-x
```

We can also employ = to replace the entire set. For example:

```
project-x members = persons [ age < 30 ]
```

Before adding the persons younger than 30, this will disassociate all previous members (unless they happen to be younger than 30) from project-x.

Both with = and <<, the inverse association changes as well. If there is a one-to-many association from item types x to y named a/b, then these two forms are synonymous:

```
x a = y
y b << x
```

The breaking of an item/subitem relationship (not an association) is equivalent to the deletion (or archiving) of the item (or items).

```
delete order-x line [ index = 0 ]
```

This removes the first line in order-x.

For associations, the following operations hold:

```
order-line-x product = none
group-x members >> person-x        // '<<' = link, '>>' = unlink
group-x members = none
```

Here, the first line breaks the relationship to a product without assigning a new one; the second removes a person as member of a group; and the last removes all members of the group.

So much for the differences between subitem relationships and associations. We don't notice these differences when querying. In the end, they are both relationships between items. Both sides have their own name, and in order to write cardinality-safe queries, we can assign each side its own singular and plural name. This means that we may have to define four names for every relationship. For example, Table 7-1 illustrates the case of orders and lines.

***Table 7-1.*** *Example of Naming Both Sides of a Relationship*

| From the Perspective of | Singular | Plural |
| --- | --- | --- |
| orders | line | lines |
| lines | order | orders |

Of course, you will only have to specify this once per relationship, and there is lots of room for shortcuts. For associations, the names of the corresponding item types can function as defaults, only to be overwritten when needed, for example, when there are multiple associations between these two types. In the same way, for subitem relationships, the parent item type can be the default for the parent-relationship. With a line item, it makes perfect sense to refer back to its parent with just order. And as in dictionaries, we might have a special syntax to easily indicate the singular and plural names, such as either line\lines or line`s, to indicate that the singular is line and the plural name is lines.

We can use a kind of data definition language (DDL; I will not be investigating this further here) to add the line subitem type to the already existing order type:

```
database order type:    // to get the order item type in scope
    new subitem:        // defines a new subitem type
        name = 'line`s'
        ...
```

This can automatically define all four names for this item/subitem relationship.

- order and orders, by automatically copying (or referring to) the name of the parent item, and;

- line and lines, from interpreting the specified line`s string

Conceptually, associations are bidirectional by definition. However, it may not always be desirable or convenient to reflect this in the data model. In the example with order lines that refer to products, it is probably not necessary to have the inverse property order-lines in the product item type, especially if there are many more associations that involve the product item type. Also, as mentioned before, when we have an association that refers to items in another system, it makes more sense to only reflect this association in the system that defines this association.

In these scenarios, it is still possible to traverse the model in the opposite direction, by inverting the query. Suppose we want to know all the months in which product-x was ordered. While we can't do this:

```
product-x order-lines orders dates months
// error: order-lines unknown
```

we can still write this:

```
orders lines [ product = product-x ] orders dates months
```

It's a matter of perspective.

- From a conceptual perspective, any relationship is bidirectional. Even if you cannot access order lines directly from a product, there still is a relationship between product and order lines. In other words, in an IR diagram, we would still draw a line between the corresponding item types.

- From a referential perspective, it may be desirable or necessary to regard some associations as unidirectional, meaning we do not always have to name the inverse relationship.

- From a technical perspective, any relationship can be implemented in any form suitable: one-sided, two-sided, a hash table, a link table, etc. The best implementation could be determined automatically or configured by the developer, but completely separate from the conceptual definition of the relationship.

# Attributes

Up until now, we mainly focused on items and relationships. There are, however, certainly a few things worth saying about the role of attributes in a set-oriented language.

Assigning a value to a singular attribute does not have to look much different from what we are used to in other languages, as in this example:

```
person name = 'John'
```

However, in a set-oriented language, the following is also feasible:

```
customers [ region = 2 ] discount = 0.05
```

Just as with a similar statement in SQL, this construct could assign the value 0.05 for all customers in the region 2.

We consciously write `discount` (singular) instead of `discounts` here. In case of a query, the plural form makes a lot of sense, but with an assignment, the singular form is more suitable. Say, we write a query to determine all discounts applied in region 2:

```
customers [ region = 2 ] discounts
```

We use the plural term here because it clearly indicates that the result of this expression is a set and not a single object. In contrast, the previous assignment example can be read as a shortened version of this *for each* loop equivalent:

```
customers [ region = 2 ]:
    discount = 0.05
```

So, even though we assign a set of attributes, it makes sense to see the actual assignment as happening within the scope of an individual item. It is not only a linguistical thing; it also makes it possible to write assignments such as

```
employees salary = salary * 1.03
```

This is possible if we also see the right-hand side of an assignment in the context of the item we assign an attribute to. Again, this is just as we would do in an explicit for each loop.

# Values vs. Items

Attributes can be used to assign values like numbers, strings, and dates but not items. For items, it is an essential property that they can be shared (referenced), while for values, this generally makes no sense. In most object-oriented languages, the difference between values and entities (items) always has been blurry. However, as you will see, there are clear advantages to making a strict distinction between the two.

Values can be seen as references to a concrete or abstract reality. A number refers to a number in an imaginary list of all possible numbers. A date refers to an entry in a once-by-humans agreed-upon calendar. A number plate, by way of a sequence of letters and numbers, refers to a vehicle. Items (typically called entities, in other modeling techniques), on the other hand, are representations of facts, for example, the fact that you consider a certain company as a customer, or the fact that this company has placed an order. But you can't record a fact without directly or indirectly referencing reality, using values. So, entities and values go hand in hand, yet they are two completely different things.

We could say that relationships are there to establish references between items (entities) within a model, and attributes exist to refer to the world outside a model.

Relationships are the reason why items are sharable by definition, in the sense that you can refer to them (internally using a key or whatever is required, but purely for the concept this does not actually matter here). The reason why it does not make sense to share values in this same way is the fact that values are references themselves. If you were able to share a value by reference as well, you would effectively be creating a so-called double indirection for no good reason (i.e., a reference to a value container that references a value). Besides this, a value on its own does not have any meaning without some form of context, such as being assigned to an attribute.

There are good reasons to be strict about this distinction between values and items. For items, an assignment or parameter passing is always by reference. For values, it is always by value. This behavior has a lot of implicit consequences. While it is possible to copy an item, a value cannot be copied explicitly. That's because, from the perspective of a value, the act of assigning a value by definition already makes a copy. And for an equals operator with items, it is logical to consider the reference itself (i.e., do they refer to the same item), while with values, it only makes sense to compare the value itself.

The fact that many object-oriented languages are not that strict in this separation has historical reasons. For example, take string classes. Because of their potentially large size and variable length, strings cannot easily be managed on a CPU's (or VM's) stack. Therefore, in object-oriented languages, it made sense to encapsulate everything to do with strings into a class. Because of this, in some languages, an unnecessary distinction exists between basic types (like numbers and characters) and strings, despite the fact that, in the end, strings are also values.

The Venn diagram in Figure 7-1 shows how the mix-up of values and sharable objects results in an in-between and inconsistent category of types.

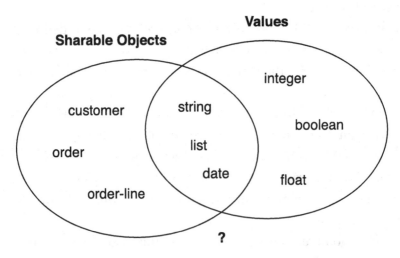

***Figure 7-1.*** *Venn diagram of sharable objects vs. values*

Having this in-between category of types has a lot of disadvantages:

- Confusion as to the meaning of the equals = operator, resulting in multiple ways to check for equality

- Workarounds, such as like `immutable`, `const`, etc., to avoid the unwanted modification of such values

- Unnecessary differences between `null` and an empty value (for instance, and empty string `""`)

This last is interesting. It is almost never necessary to functionally distinguish between a string variable not being assigned and an empty string (`""`), yet this distinction exists in many programming languages, leading to a lot of extra code to check both cases—all this while integers, floats, and other basic types (at least in statically typed languages) often cannot be optionally valued, even though that could be very useful from time to time.

We should, and can, get rid of this unnatural and archaic distinction by making a strict one between values and items. By putting things such as strings, dates, etc., into the category of values, we give them strict and clear value semantics and get rid of the confusion that is typical in so many languages.

It is important to see that this is only about the separation of by-value and by-reference behavior. It does not mean that values cannot have properties or methods associated with them. In other words, both values and items can be regarded as objects. This makes it possible to write such things as

```
12 factorial
```

```
today month first-day
```

in which

- `factorial()` is a function inside the integer value type

- `month()` is a function of a date value

- `first-day()` is a function within the month value type

The fact that we consider values as non-sharable does not mean they cannot be handled internally by reference, either for performance or practical reasons, typically, because of the variable length (e.g., strings) or sheer size of such a value (e.g., images). That, however, does not detract from the conceptual side of it.

Besides predefined values, such as numbers, strings, and the like, it is also possible for you to define your own value types, such as a point with an x and a y coordinate.

```
define-value-type point:
    x as number
    y as number
```

---

**Note**    This is a pseudo syntax, given only as an example.

---

The x and the y in this example are attributes of a new value type, point, which can subsequently be used as a value type for attributes.

Apart from attributes, a value type might also support unidirectional associations, like currency in this example:

```
define-value-type monetary-amount:
    currency -> database currency
    value as number
```

Here, we combine a reference to a separate currency table with a number, to allow us to easily exchange monetary values within an application.

# Putting It All Together

Let's sum up all aspects of the IR model thus far.

In the IR model, entities are called items. All items are part of an ownership hierarchy in which every item, except for the root item, is a subitem of another item. A database is represented by an item itself, which acts as the root of the hierarchy, just as the root directory in a file system is itself a directory. Item/subitem relationships are always one-to-many or one-to-one, and they form a composition, in the sense that subitems are deleted (archived) when their parent item is deleted.

We call non-subitem relationships associations. Associations are relationships that by definition are not compositional. So, they can intersect the ownership-hierarchy. While, conceptually, associations are always bidirectional, we do recognize unidirectional associations, in which case, we do not specify the inverse relationship.

Attributes may be defined in terms of value types, such as numbers and strings, but it is also possible to define your own value types. Such a self-defined type can consist of attributes and unidirectional associations.

The schema in Figure 7-2 illustrates the different types of properties.

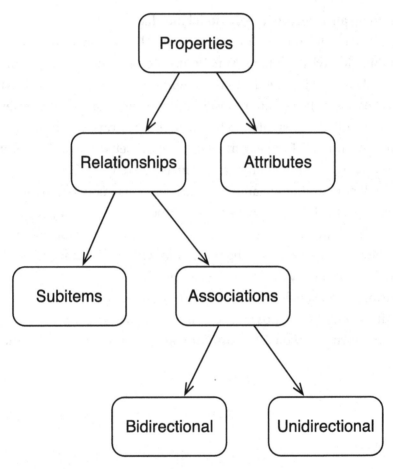

***Figure 7-2.*** *Types of properties*

The differences between items and values can be listed as follows (Table 7-2).

***Table 7-2.***  *Differences Between Items and Values*

|  | **Items** | **Values** |
| --- | --- | --- |
| Assignment | By reference | By value |
| Assignable to | Associations | Attributes |
| Shared | Yes | No |
| May be copied | Yes | Assignment implies copying |
| Type definition | Indirectly, by the definition of a subitem | By way of a separate definition |
| Possible properties | Attributes Subitems Associations | Attributes Unidirectional associations |

For items, it holds that the definition of a subitem defines both the type and the relationship. These are inseparable. When defining them you specify the following:

- The name of the subitem, both in singular and plural form

- The cardinality, either singular (1) or multiple (N)

- Whether the subitem is optional or mandatory

- *Optional*: The name of the inverse relationship (the reference to the parent), both in singular and plural form. If this is omitted, the name of the parent item type is used by default.

The cardinality and optionality of the inverse relationship (from subitem to its parent) does not have to be set, because it is always singular and mandatory.

For bidirectional associations, we specify

- The name of the relationship, both in singular and plural form. By default, this is the name of the item type referring to.

- The name of the inverse relationship, both in singular and plural form. By default, this is the name of the item type referring back to.

- The cardinality of both sides of the relationship

- Whether the relationship is optional or mandatory, again for both sides of the relationship

As an aside, despite the use of the term *inverse relationship*, both sides of a bidirectional relationship are considered equivalent.

For unidirectional associations, we specify

- The name of the relationship, both in singular and plural form. By default, this is the name of the item type referring to.

- The cardinality of the relationship

- Whether the relationship is optional or mandatory

For attributes, we must specify

- The name of the attribute, both in singular and plural form

- The value type

- The cardinality (in case multi-valued attributes are supported)

- Whether the attribute is optional or mandatory

Both items and values are objects, in the sense that you can define associated member methods (functions and procedures) with them. The object inheritance hierarchy could look like that in Figure 7-3.

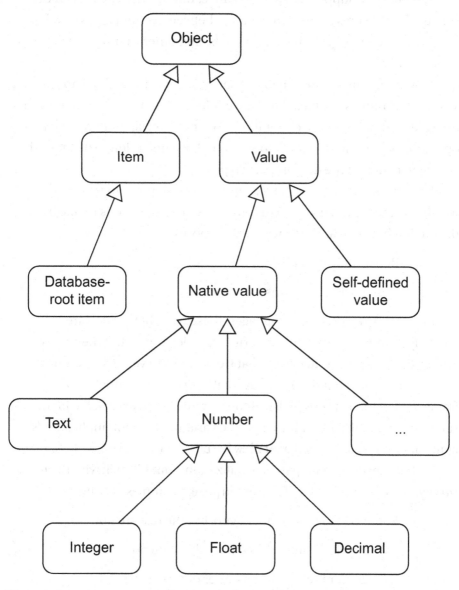

***Figure 7-3.*** *Base types inheritance hierarchy*

# Inheritance?

The inheritance hierarchy in the previous section (Figure 7-3) reveals that the IR model can support class inheritance. Inheritance can indeed be very useful to express common behavior between certain types of values, such as between integers, floats, decimals, and other values. But what about items?

Although it sounds logical to support item-type inheritance too, at first sight, it contradicts the idea that the definition of item types coincides with the definition of the property for that subitem in its parent item. The new operator, as presented so far, also seems to have no option to distinguish between instance type and property type.

The solution to this dilemma is in looking into the actual intentions we have using inheritance. In computer sciences, one tends to make a distinction between at least these two purposes:

- Reuse another type

- Define specializations (subtypes)

In most object-oriented languages, these two phenomena are typically covered with a single inheritance mechanism, but they are two totally different beasts. Reuse is what we may use if we want a variation of something that already exists, say, making your own subclass of a framework class. This is typically done by reusing the base behavior of such a class and then creating a specific variation for your application's context, for example, a `CustomerView` based on a general `View` class.

In that sense, subtyping (or specializations, but I'll stick with the term *subtyping* from here) has a different purpose. Examples of subtypes are

- Some employees are managers but the rest are not.

- Some projects are finished but others are not.

- A customer is either a consumer or a business.

These examples already reflect one aspect of subtyping that is different from reuse, and that's the fact that a subtype can change. An employee can become a manager; a project is first started and then finished. Object-oriented programming languages are not really equipped to reflect something like the latter with subclasses. And that's not even a problem, because they only manipulate volatile in-memory data. But with persistent data, it suddenly becomes a need to change an item's subtype over time.

Another difference with reuse is that an object could *be* (!) multiple subtypes at the same time. Think about a person who is both a *manager* and *highly educated*. If both imply some additional properties, then these *states*, as we call them, certainly apply as subtypes, but they can, of course, occur together. Something like that is also not covered by most object-oriented programming languages.

Maybe it is better to think about subtypes as roles or predicates. We could even regard them as a special kind of Boolean attribute (is-manager, is-finished) that implies other attributes to be applicable or not. Looking at subtypes in this way means we can broadly generalize the concept.

We could define constraints as to whether certain states (i.e., subtypes) can occur together or not.

- A project could be finished only after it is started (logical implication).

- A customer is either a consumer or a business (logical exclusive).

We can even stretch the concept of subtypes to resemble something of enum types. Let's say we have a set of items that represent product groups, and we want to refer to specific product groups in our business logic. These things happen a lot in software applications. It's when instances in the database get sort of *bound* to pieces of business logic. Given that we can mark certain product groups by making them of a certain subtype, we can use that from within the concerning business logic. If we uniquely associate each product group with a single predicate (a certain attribute being `true`), then we have effectively created an enumeration that is backed by actual database instances.

It does not have to be that we integrate all these concepts, but looking at it from such an angle shows how all these concepts are tightly related to the base type to which they apply. So, instead of looking at them as isolated subclasses, we could look at subtypes as additions to the base type, meaning that you define them in the item type they apply to. This might break with the taboo against a base type being dependent on a subtype, but there is nothing wrong with a project type knowing that, when finished, it has some additional attributes, such as a finished date. We can define such attributes within the subtype, for example, as here:

```
database
    subitem customer
        name as text
        subtype consumer
            birth-date as date
        subtype business
            registration-number as number
```

This solves the dilemma of subtyping for items. Now what about reuse?

The IR model could support reuse by making it possible to base a new item type on an existing item type. For example, like this:

```
my-database
    subitem my-orders based-on other-database order
```

This would automatically transfer all properties and behaviors of the order type in `other-database` (I won't go into detail here on how to refer to other database schemas, but that's one way of reusing a type). As with inheritance in general, we would be able to add additional properties and methods or even overwrite specific behavior. The good thing is that given the versioned schemas of both databases, we can still keep control over what version will be the basis of our own `my-order` type.

If we add an attribute `priority` to `my-order`, we can then do this:

```
my-database:
    new my-order:
        date = today  // reused attribute
        priority = 2  // added attribute
```

However, how would this work for relationships? They would refer to types in the base model. If we create our own orders, we probably also want to create our own associated order lines. And even when the mechanism makes sure new `my-order` lines are created in `my-database` and not the `other-database`, the question remains: What happens if we want to create our own variant of lines and add an additional attribute at that level?

```
new my-order:
    date = today
    priority = 2
    new line:
        count = 10
        discount = 5%  // added attribute
        ...
```

This is actually a common dilemma in object-oriented programming. When subclassing multiple classes from a framework, the references between those classes do not automatically follow the types you define yourself. That's because inheritance is seen as a class-oriented concept. Obviously, the `lines` property could be polymorphous, in the sense that it can hold your own `my-line` instances, but a language can only understand a query like this:

```
my-order-x lines discounts maximum
```

if it knows that the returned lines are a variant of the original line type. Obviously, a dynamic language can cope with this at runtime, but the IR model is a statically typed concept for a reason.

Fortunately, the IR model can shine a new light on this subject. The solution could be something similar to this:

1. When basing an item type on a previously defined item type, you do not just inherit that single item type. Instead, you also inherited the whole item sub-tree that is below that type.

2. The item/subitem relationships automatically adapt to reflect the new types.

3. Even associations that refer from within that tree to another item type in that same tree will adapt.

Rules 1 and 2 mean that, given the example, after reusing an order type from another database model, we automatically get a shadow line type that comes with it, just because line is defined as a subitem of order.

Rule 3 means that, given the same example, if we want to reuse a complete order administration from another model, we should start basing an item type on that level. If that includes the product item type, the lines will automatically refer to your own automatically subclassed product item type.

This idea just extends the concept of class inheritance into a kind of framework inheritance. What to do with associations that go outside the inherited tree stays unanswered, but knowing that a certain item tree will be reused by others, of course, also brings the obligation to refrain from external dependencies anyway. And maybe the IR model could give us some escape to overwrite particular external associations to get somewhat more control over these otherwise loose ends.

Certainly, these ideas are very early stage, and we will not explore them any further here now. But it is an interesting subject, which is why it is included here.

# Summary

At its core, the IR model I've defined here is an ER model, but with a number of additions. On the one hand, this is to make it more universal and suitable to serve as a database schema and, on the other hand, to make queries and updates expressed in terms of the model more suitable to be integrated into a programming language.

In contrast with most database architectures, the IR model incorporates relationships as first-class citizens. This allows us to leave technical details such as foreign keys and linking tables up to the internal implementation of the database engine, while at the same time giving us a natural way to refer to relationships from within queries.

The IR model combines a number of well-known concepts.

- Just as in hierarchical databases and JSON/XML documents, it recognizes that ownership between entities is virtually always hierarchical.

- As with SQL, it strictly separates the conceptual model from the underlying implementation and configuration.

- Like object databases, it considers items (entities) as objects, with properties, functions, and local scope.

- Similar to AppleScript, it recognizes that the use of singular and plural names is beneficial to the readability of queries.

The concept of subitems simplifies the model, because it combines a number of things.

- It defines the item/subitem relationships themselves.

- It classifies those relationships as an ownership composition.

- It implicitly defines the type of the subitem, alleviating the need for a separate class hierarchy.

- It provides local scope for new operations.

- It serves as an implicit package name qualifier.

The conceptual approach of the IR model not only makes the physical storage less dependent on the schema, it also helps to optimize query execution. As in SQL, queries in terms of the IR model can be seen as specifications as to what is requested, rather than how to execute them. This is not limited to a single query. It can be extended to entire service requests, as you will see in the next chapter.

The IR model is not just suitable for purely database applications. In theory, lots of systems can be modeled in terms of an IR model. Think of an industrial machine that can represent itself as an IR-based data source with the purpose of monitoring its behavior. Even a file system could be modeled as an IR model, in which case, a query like this might determine the total amount of bytes consumed by big files in backup directories:

```
directories recursive [ name = 'backup' ]
    files [ size > 1 megabyte ] sizes sum
```

Even an SQL mapper is not out of the question. Where it is traditionally very difficult to prevent unwanted lazy loading with object-relational mapping tools, we can avoid this with IR modeling, by employing the principles of implicit services, as described in the next chapter. This means we will only require a single round-trip to retrieve any arbitrary combination of data.

Having explained the basics of the IR model, I am now ready to elaborate on the concept of implicit services.

# CHAPTER 8

# Implicit Services

*The first rule of any technology used in a business is that automation applied to an efficient operation will magnify the efficiency. The second is that automation applied to an inefficient operation will magnify the inefficiency.*

—Bill Gates

Now that you've been introduced to the IR model and the accompanying query language in the last two chapters, you have a basis to delve deeper into the idea of implicit services. The concept of implicit services consists of a generic API that a client can use to access data on a server, without having to explicitly implement every possible request beforehand, as would be the case with service-oriented architectures (SOAs). At its core, an implicit service request is a set of queries. So, we could call it a query API. However, as you will see shortly, a generic service API goes much further than a typical database query API.

The biggest advantage of implicit services is that they do not require code to be written for run-of-the-mill CRUD operations. Immediately after you have defined a data model, you can issue any request from the client to add, change, delete, or query data. With the proper client software, these requests can even be deduced from screen definitions. This puts the client application developer back into the driver's seat. In that sense, implicit services not only save a lot on development, they also ease the dependencies between developers or even between projects.

© Jos Jong 2019
J. Jong, *Vertically Integrated Architectures*,
https://doi.org/10.1007/978-1-4842-4252-0_8

By way of fine-grained authorizations, we can prevent a client from receiving unwarranted access to certain data. This is, of course, mostly relevant for calls stemming from an external system. Constraints and database triggers, in addition, ensure that a client cannot apply mutations that go against the design of the system.

Implicit service calls do not have to be limited to CRUD operations. In a service request, a client may refer to functions that are defined within the IR data model. This helps us to put reusable business logic at the level of the database server, whether it is a simple calculation or an elaborate construct of queries and other functions. The same goes for update operations, for which you may define a procedure as part of the IR model, as with an SQL stored procedure, but more lightweight.

Obviously, the concept of implicit services is not entirely new. So-called *backend as a service* (BaaS) solutions seek to prevent the need to write basic CRUD operations in a similar fashion. But these, often REST-based, solutions frequently bog down on the idea that you mainly want to exchange lists of similar records or documents with the server. With the concept of implicit services, as proposed in this chapter, we take things a step further.

# Perfect Granularity

When developing an SOA environment, the granularity of services, in the sense of the trade-off between course- and fine-grained, can be quite a design dilemma. Implicit services are not subject to this dilemma, because it is the client that determines what data must be exchanged—perfect granularity, you could say.

You might think that this holds for any client that has direct access to a database. After all, every database API gives you complete freedom to retrieve any data you need, by way of a generic query language or protocol. But it is not that simple. For example, it is often not possible (or is too cumbersome) to combine queries into a single server call, resulting in multiple network round-trips. Some, especially REST or document-based, databases may return whole documents, even though you are interested only in a single value from a document.

We can only speak of perfect granularity if a client can retrieve all the data it needs (a) in a single network round-trip, (b) for any arbitrary subset of data, which (c) includes derived data, and (d) without receiving unnecessary data.

By definition, an SQL query always returns a two-dimensional table. This makes it impossible to return hierarchical structures, such as, for example, customer data including all related orders. Some SQL products had implemented their own extensions to support multiple queries in a single request, but this never became widely popular.

Most NoSQL databases have similar limitations for combining queries. There are those that have *join*-like features (like lookup in MongoDB) to slightly reduce the number of network round-trips, but this does not suffice for every imaginable combination of data requests. Regardless, many document-based (JSON) databases return entire documents, for which reason they fail to satisfy requirement (d).

A standardized REST interface such as Microsoft Dynamics OData (www.odata.org) is a valiant attempt to provide a generic query-like interface. But REST, in general, assumes a single entity (item type) per end point. As a result, such solutions do not really satisfy conditions (a) and (b).

The importance of having a single round-trip must not be underestimated. No matter how fast we make the internal components of a system, once we start communicating between physically separated subsystems, for example, between client and server, a single round-trip can take up to 100ms. There is no way to overcome this limitation, because it is limited by the speed of light. Besides, even when client and server are in close proximity of each other, we still have to deal with the overhead of individual network calls.

In practice, this means that we have to make sure that we limit the maximum number of network calls resulting from a single user action. It may be acceptable to retrieve data per item type, but as soon as we call a service for each instance of a given item type, we're in a danger zone, as far as response times are concerned. This is what is known as the so-called lazy loading issue with ORM tools, in which on-demand database queries can precipitate a storm of network calls when not tuned wisely. It is also grounds for the dilemma between fine-grained and course-grained services: reusability vs. performance. It also made CORBA and J2EE entity beans not perform in real-world settings.

True, the total response time of a system may be reduced by submitting queries in parallel and asynchronously processing their results. But that's only a feasible option as long as queries don't depend on one another. Especially if you have to retrieve *related data*, you definitely need the results from an earlier query (for example, in the form of keys) to perform the next. This gives rise to synchronous behavior, in which multiple round-trips can again add up to unnecessary or even unacceptable response times.

The only real solution is a protocol that allows the processing of an arbitrary combination of queries, related or not, with a single round-trip. For this to happen, we must stop thinking in terms of retrieving records or documents and make sure we support any type of desired result, no matter how large or hierarchical its structure.

We can employ the query language illustrated in the previous chapters to describe such an implicit service. Let's see how that might look like.

# The Service Request

Suppose we want to retrieve all `invoices` of a `customer` with `id` 123. The basis of such a service request would be the following query:

```
customer [ id = 123 ] invoices
```

The question, however, is what the server should return. Should it be all attributes of those invoices? Perhaps also the invoice lines? Or just the keys of the invoices?

The trick is to stop thinking in terms of records. We can just specify exactly which attributes we want to be returned.

```
customer [ id = 123 ] invoices:
    :: number
    :: date
```

With which we mean:

- Find the customer with id 123 in the database.

- Find the invoices of that customer.

- Per invoice, return the number and date fields.

The indentation after a colon is a kind of for each here, as we have seen before. The symbol : :, in this context, indicates what attributes to return, again, merely as a way of explaining the concept presented here, not to describe a specific definition language.

But we don't have to limit ourselves to attributes. The following is possible as well:

```
customer [ id = 123 ] invoices:
    :: number
    :: date
    :: lines amounts sum
```

In addition to the invoice number and date, this service now returns the outcome of the expression lines amounts sum, being the total amount of the invoice.

While an IR model consists of items, relationships, and attributes with values, in the end, it is only values that can be returned in a response. The items and relationships are abstract concepts that only manifest themselves indirectly, by way of nested structures. An item may be represented by returning its key (e.g., automatically generated by the database; we will ignore this for now), but even that is an attribute and, thus, a value.

We now have the groundwork for retrieving data, but so far, only for single expressions in the context of a single item type, just as in SQL, in which you can only return a sequence of column values together forming a two-dimensional table. And that will not get us to perfect granularity.

The solution is to accept nested queries, such as with lines, in this example:

```
customer [ id = 123 ] invoices:
    :: number
    :: date
    lines:
        :: product name
        :: amount
```

The result of this query now is a hierarchical structure. It does not only contain the number and date per invoice but also, per invoice, a nested list of lines with a product name, and amount for each line.

We can also include functions, such as in this example:

```
customers [ region = 4 ]:
    :: name
    invoices sort(date) last(5):
        :: date
        :: amount
```

For each customer in region 4, this query returns the name and the last five of its invoices, in terms of their date and amount.

Besides nesting, query expressions can also specify more than one subquery on the same level. If, for example, for a customer, we want both his/her overdue invoices and contact-persons, we may formulate this as follows:

```
customer [ id = 123 ]:
    :: name
    invoices [ not payed and due-date < today ]:
        :: date
        :: amount
    contact-persons:
        :: name
```

Of course, we can also allow this at the root level of a service request. So, if we want to both retrieve certain customers and all products in the database, we may specify this as follows:

```
customers [ region = 4 ]:
    :: name
products:
    :: id
    :: name
```

Elements of what we just discussed are not new, of course. Something like GraphQL (http://graphql.org/) comes close. However, the IR model is not limited to querying a specific kind of data, such as JSON documents, and owing to the full integration with an accompanying programming language, we can benefit from such things as property chaining, user defined functions, etc.

# Access Control

In a traditional SOA-based application, access control is achieved by a combination of service design, URL authorizations, and program logic. The service design makes sure that we only return or update data as agreed. URL authorizations can limit the client's access to a subset of the API. And we can use program logic to make any exception we require, depending on the user and the data itself.

However, with implicit services, there is no such a thing as a service-specific implementation that we can put logic into. Because the client can submit any request it wants through the generic API, we require some other way to selectively grant or deny access.

The solution is to put access control directly on top of the data model, so that we can specify the authorization for users and user groups in terms of that same data model. In a way, this does not appear to be different from what most databases are already capable of. There *is* a difference, however. Contrary to their original intent, traditional databases are typically put behind an application server. This leads to a situation in which all database access is done with a single user account, which means that the access control support of databases becomes kind of useless. In a VIA architecture, we do not have this separation between application server and database. This means that with the help of an integrated (possibly pluggable) user management system, the server can know the exact origin of every service request, even to the level of the end user.

We can use this to put in place a fine-grained authorization model, in which we can grant and deny access to each individual item, relationship, and attribute, depending on user groups. And by making it possible to specify a logical expression, we can also grant data based on user-specific data.

Also, thanks to this level of integration, we can design the programming language to automatically deduce the authorization for derived data from the underlying database elements. For example, suppose we define a function age() that determines a person's age based on their `date-of-birth`. Then, if a certain user is not allowed to access this `date-of-birth` attribute, we can automatically cascade this to not allow him/her access to the function `age()`, unless, of course, we decide to deviate from this default behavior.

Such an authorization-aware programming environment also gives us the opportunity to hugely improve the handling of authorization exceptions. Instead of crashing the entire service execution and returning a stack trace, it can return a neat *no access* indicator value, not just for the entire service response, but only at the level of the attributes concerned. In other words, if you are not authorized for certain data or data elements, this does not lead to a failing service request. Instead, it returns all data that you do have access to, together with information about the data elements to which you were not granted access. If we then add a generic client runtime that knows how to handle these exceptions, the whole setup would be less prone to errors, just as with the partial execution in a spreadsheet program in which certain calculation errors will not withhold the program to calculate all other formulas, and certainly not crash the spreadsheet program.

## Update vs. Read Services

In SOA, the distinction between query and update services is a matter of design. In VIA, we can explicitly separate the two. Because of the generic interface, we could than say that we have

- A single generic read service—for all data retrieval requests

- A single generic write service—for all update requests

This clear separation comes with a number of advantages. A read service request is a specification as to which data must be retrieved, while a write service request looks rather like an update script. Because of this difference, we can give the read service the characteristics of a pure functional (lambda) function. We can then be sure that there are no side effects, which allows the implementation to do full query optimizations without affecting the result. It also means that a read service request is always idempotent and that, thus, the client may repeat the exact same call as it pleases, without consequences, for example, for doing a refresh in the event of network issues.

The write service has none of these characteristics. As said, a write request can act more like a script, as in this example, which adds a new order.

```
customer [ id = 123 ]:
    new order:
        date = today
        new line:
            product = product [ id = 456 ]
            count = 1
            price = product price * .95
```

This brings the database from one state to another. It is because of this that the client should be informed whether this was successful. We are now in the realm of transactions. In most cases, it will be logical to view a singular write service call as a unit of work and, thus, as a single transaction. Perhaps for batch-like processing it is possible to conceive of transaction demarcation over multiple calls, but we'll disregard this for now.

# Schema Evolution vs. Service Versioning

A data model is the foundation of every software system. This is why it frequently can be subject to changes when adding new features. Every modification of the data model may have consequences for existing databases and external systems; therefore, it is not enough to regard model changes as a simple *diff* between two versions of a model, as we would do with a text file comparison in Git. It might be necessary to develop a migration script for existing test and production databases. And if a system offers services to external systems or to a client that cannot be updated on the fly (like a native mobile client), we must ensure that the service API is backward-compatible.

What is interesting about this phenomenon is that a parallel can be drawn between migrating an old database and supporting an older version of a client. Let's illustrate this with an example.

Imagine that an existing system contains an item type called `customer` with an optional attribute `region`. Then, say we want this attribute to become mandatory. There are three aspects concerned with such a migration:

1. What to do with existing records for which the attribute region is empty

2. The adaption of the actual (not `null`) constraint on the database schema

3. How to deal with updates from an old client (UI or external system) that does not provide a value for region

With regard to (1), let's assume we want to assign the value 9 to all these customers. To solve (1) we could then execute this statement:

```
customers [ region = none ] region = 9
```

This assigns the value 9 to all `customers` that did not have a region assigned. After this, we could add the constraint to solve (2).

To resolve (3), we could have a mechanism that automatically replaces the incoming missing `region` values with the value 9.

In SQL, to cover these same three aspects, we would execute the following statements:

```
(1) UPDATE CUSTOMER SET REGION = 9 WHERE REGION = NULL
```

```
(2) ALTER TABLE CUSTOMER ALTER COLUMN REGION NOT NULL
```

```
(3) ALTER TABLE CUSTOMER ALTER COLUMN REGION DEFAULT 9
```

What becomes apparent from this is that we can draw a parallel between (1) and (3). In a manner of speaking, until one second before the migration, a client could have put the value NULL in region. It is, therefore, more than logical that a later call with a NULL value is also translated into the value 9.

What this boils down to is that being compatible with an old database and being compatible with write service requests from an older client (not reads, I'll get back to that in the next section) are essentially the same: they are both concerned with backward-compatibility against data that is defined in terms of an older version of the data model. That is an invitation to devise a common strategy for this.

We may view it as a mapping between an old and a new data model. We then get a much more *functional* approach, compared to an imperative UPDATE (SQL) statement. A schema migration becomes a lambda that the server can use for both migrating stored data and handling write requests from an outdated client. Such a mapping can come out of every conceivable combination of expressions for as long as there are no side effects, which enables the server to execute them without consequences, whenever necessary.

What is special about such a mapping is that the incoming and outgoing data are based on another version of the data model. Suppose, staying with the earlier example, that we write the following mapping (pseudo code):

```
region =
    if region = none:
        return 9
    else:
        return region
```

The first line with `region` = here refers to the `region` attribute in the new schema. Wherever `region` is referenced later on, this is in terms of the old schema. We could read it as follows (again pseudo code, not meant to be a formal syntax):

```
region~new =
    if region~old = none:
        return 9
    else:
        return region~old
```

This is kind of similar to how, with SQL database triggers, you can refer to the old and new values of an assignment (before and after values), with the important distinction, of course, that it is not about the value but about the differently defined variants of an attribute.

As said, the syntax here should be taken with a grain of salt. It just tries to illustrate the concept. We are probably better off defining such mappings with a specialized tool, not just with a piece of source code. This tool can also know when a mapping is needed, and it can register the relationship of a mapping with the model change with which it is concerned. The whole point is that these mappings interact with the versioning of the data model. So, we are bridging metadata with software versioning here.

Let's present a slightly more complex scenario now—one in which we change the cardinality of a relationship. In the model in Figure 8-1, every customer is associated with a single address.

**Figure 8-1.** *Single address per customer*

Now, suppose we want to start registering multiple addresses per customer, as in Figure 8-2.

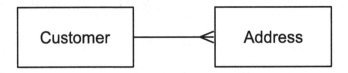

**Figure 8-2.** *One or more addresses per customer*

We also want to introduce an additional attribute `type` on `address` and decide that there may be multiple `addresses`, but there can only be one main address, and we indicate this with `type` = `main`. We then define the following mapping within the context of `customer`.

`addresses = set ( address )`

and within the context of address:

`type = main`

In this case, the mapping consists of two lambdas. The first means that the single `address` from the old situation in the new situations becomes an `address` in a set of `addresses` (in the next section, you will see that this can also be done implicitly). The second mapping says that the new field called `type` must initially be filled with the value `main`.

It is not the intention here to detail all aspects of such a mechanism. There are some challenges to mold all possible conversions in such a form. But if we succeed, this gives us a number of interesting things.

First, the mapping can be used for automatic database migrations. Every database that we run against a newer version of an application can be converted automatically to the applicable version of the schema.

As said before, it also ensures that all write service requests are automatically handled in a backward-compatible way. The server may first convert each of those requests to the reigning schema and, only then, apply the current business logic.

The latter is actually of much more fundamental advantage than the first. We need a backward-compatibility mechanism, in one way or another. Because implicit services free us from writing explicit service implementations, this has to be in a way that is not bound to a specific type of request. In this sense, it is an essential ingredient to realize the concept of implicit services.

We could even take it a step further. One of the biggest objections to the two-tier architecture, as was the adage in the nineties, was the direct dependency of client applications on the database model. This dependency poses a problem with certain types of schema migrations. The easiest way out was to always distribute a new client with every change, but that was not always practical (web clients only came into the scene later). Services resolved this problem, as they allowed full control over the external exposition of system modifications. The high price we've paid for this, however, is that we have to manually write the boilerplate code for each and every read and write operation, including basic CRUD operations.

# Inverse Schema Mappings

You've just seen how we can draw a parallel between database migrations and backward-compatibility of services; however, that does not cover the entire spectrum of possible data model changes. We'll do that now. Some modifications are relatively easy to deal with, although this depends on how well they are handled by the client and server. You will also learn that it is sometimes necessary to define an inverse mapping.

Let's start with a relatively simple migration: changing the name of an item, relationship, or attribute. Even though this may be very desirable for reasons of clarity once in a while, in practice, there is a tendency to defer such changes as long as possible, because of the benefits not outweighing the effort of writing a database migration and writing code to distinguish different variations of a service call. Fortunately, with implicit services, there may be less of a dilemma. Let's assume we require every client to indicate which version of the data model a request is based on. With that knowledge, the server knows exactly what attribute, item, or relationship a certain name refers to, and it can also respond with the correct names—all without writing any code. This means we no longer have to agonize over name changes, which can benefit code readability and maintainability in general.

A more radical solution to cope with name changes would be to refer to data elements with a unique id instead of a name. The tools we use could translate these internal ids to the actual names and vice versa. Technically, this could work fine, for example, with a binary protocol between client and server and a fully integrated tool set. On the other hand, it is probably not a viable approach for external systems that don't integrate with this tool set.

Besides renaming elements or very specific data transformations, a lot of data model changes are typically about adding new data elements, such as a new item, relationship, or attribute. Although such additions seemingly do not have so much impact, this actually depends on the associated constraints. The introduction of a new attribute could be backward-compatible with older clients and older databases, but not if this attribute is declared as a mandatory field. The same would hold true for a new relationship that is very much compatible unless it is a mandatory relationship. And it is not only when we add data elements. A change of a constraint itself can also either be backward-compatible or not. It actually depends on whether we read or write data.

In a way, it is only the constraints that a model enforces onto a client or database that determines whether a model is backward-compatible with older data or not. The structure of a model is describing a universe of potential data structures, but it is the constraints that limit this to a certain subset of that universe.

What all this boils down to is that we can categorize a lot of data model changes as either tightening a constraint (i.e., less values accepted), or relaxing a constraint (i.e., more values accepted). As stated previously, whether the tightening or the relaxation of constraints requires a schema mapping depends on which direction the data flows (read or write service).

When a constraint is tightened, it may be that existing data in a database or data sent by an existing client no longer complies with this constraint. This is exactly the type of scenario on which I centered the discussion in the previous section. We need to cater to the following scenarios:

- An optional attribute becoming mandatory

- An optional relationship (either association or item/ subitem) becoming mandatory

- A plural relationship (either association or item/ subitem) becoming singular

- A new mandatory attribute being added

- A new mandatory relationship (either association or item/subitem) being added

When relaxing constraints, the exact opposite happens. The scenarios relevant in this case are

- A mandatory attribute becoming optional

- A mandatory relationship (either association or item/ subitem) becoming optional

- A singular relationship (either association or item/subitem) becoming plural

- An attribute being removed

- A relationship (either association or item/subitem) being removed

Because existing data satisfies relaxed constraints by definition, we do not have to migrate any data in such a case. For the same reason, relaxed constraints never pose a problem to process a client's write request.

For data flowing from server to client (reading data), it does not matter whether constraints were tightened, because the client has been built with more relaxed constraints in mind, anyway. So, it is still perfectly capable of processing and showing that data. In contrast to that, when constraints are relaxed, a client can be confronted with empty fields or missing relationships, where it was expecting them to have a value. So, we need a solution for that, for example, with a mapping that is in the opposite direction as what is described in the previous section, an inversed mapping.

This reasoning is summarized in the following schema (Table 8-1):

***Table 8-1.***  *Mappings Needed Depending On Scenario*

|  | **Tightening Constraints** | **Relaxing Constraints** |
| --- | --- | --- |
| (a) Database based on old schema | Mapping needed (old to new) | - |
| (b) Old client writes data to server | Mapping needed (old to new) | - |
| (c) Old client reads data from server | - | Mapping needed (new to old) |

Both (a) and (b) have been discussed in the previous section, because of the parallel that exists between the two. For both of these, we map from and old schema to a new schema. With (c), we now have an inverse scenario, in which we must map from a new schema to an old schema.

Let's go back to the earlier example concerned with the relationship between customers and addresses. In retrospect, this has, with the insights from the preceding, both a tightening and a relaxing aspect.

- *Relaxing*: The cardinality of the relationship between customer and address goes from one (1) to many (N).

- *Tightening*: A new attribute type in address is mandatory.

Strictly speaking, the relaxed cardinality does not require a database migration. It may very well be that the database physically stores a singular relationship differently than a multi-valued one. So, it might still be that the database has to do a conversion (once, or on the fly). But that is an internal matter. Purely from a conceptual view, the only thing happening here is that the maximum-one-address-per-customer constraint is lifted. As a result, we actually do not have to write this mapping presented in the previous section:

```
addresses~new = set(address~old)
```

The database can figure out this mapping by itself. Another way of looking at this is that a single address can be implicitly regarded as a set of addresses (although only consisting of one) within a context in which a set of addresses is expected. This is one of the benefits of dealing with sets as first-class citizens instead of having to deal with instances of collection classes vs. object references.

But remember, this only works for the database migration and write requests. For read operations, we must specify an inverse mapping that could look like this:

```
address~old = addresses~new [ type = main ] first
```

The effect of this mapping is that an old client only gets to see the main address and not the other ones. That is, of course, a concession to a certain degree. But that's a design decision, and a price we have to pay anyway, whether we apply the concept of implicit services or not.

## Mapping Exemptions

Defining mappings for data model changes sounds like a lot of work. Actually, however, there are a lot of scenarios that don't require any mapping at all.

For example, say that no external system has access to our data model while the application's own client is always kept up to date, as would be the case with a stand-alone web application. In such a case, we never have to specify any inverse mapping, because it never requires a transformation from a new schema back to an old schema.

Then again, if we do allow access to external systems, we might just limit our focus to the data structures accessed by these systems. At first glance, this seems to contradict the idea of a generic query API, in which the client can access any data it wants. But, fortunately, there are a few things that can help us in this respect. First, the system could keep a record of which parts of the model are accessed remotely (in production). Second, we can use the authorization mechanism in place. If we only gave the concerning remote systems a partial view on the data model, we do not have to bother for any inverse mappings outside that scope.

Another way to reduce the need for mapping is to define a number of generic rules as to how a client should deal with certain types of model changes. An outdated UI client may very well show an empty value (or -, or something similar), if a field goes from being mandatory to optional.

The reverse is possible if a constraint has been tightened, for example, when an optional attribute becomes mandatory. We can bolster the implicit service protocol with an option for the server to return a generic field-level validation error that a client's generic framework may show to the user. This would enable users of the older client to still comply with the tightened constraint.

# Summary

A substantial part of this chapter on implicit services was concerned with the granularity and version management of services. That's because these are the essential pillars this concept is based on.

By striving for perfect granularity, we get rid of whatever reason to split service requests. Most database APIs and query languages are centered on querying tables, table results, or documents, which may require the client to perform extra network calls. This doesn't have to be the end of the world, but in some cases, we, as programmers, have to account for this, meaning we have to write specific code to work around this, which would interfere with the idea of implicit services.

By viewing an implicit service request as a tree of expressions and subqueries, we can eliminate this problem completely. There no longer is the risk of a performance hit, owing to unexpected lazy loading behavior between client and server. But, and this can be seen as an added bonus, the server is able to perform a complete optimization of the entire request. I'll return to this in the next chapter, on a persistence-aware programming language.

You've also seen that a parallel can be drawn between the version management of a data model and the backward-compatibility of services. A client sending data that assumes an older version of the data model, for that reason, can be dealt with similarly to a database that has not been migrated from that same data model version. We can utilize this similarity to get rid of explicit migration scripts and backward-compatible service implementations. Instead, we can define mappings to translate data from one version of a model to the next.

When required, we can also define inverse mappings, in order to respond to read requests of an outdated client. As we have seen, many changes are implicitly backward-compatible, so we only have to do this for certain types of changes.

In addition to these discussions on granularity and version management, we've concluded that the separation between read and write requests can be very helpful, if only because they show very different behavior in the event of a failure, but it will also help the server to fully optimize a service request. I will go into some more detail on this in the next chapter.

The following chapter explores the idea of a persistence-aware programming language. In light of vertical integration, there is plenty to be said on how such a language could look.

# CHAPTER 9

# Persistence-Aware Programming

*Computer languages differ not so much in what they make possible, but in what they make easy.*

—Larry Wall

The vertically integrated architecture advocated in this book rests on three pillars:

- A unified conceptual data model

- Implicit services

- A persistence-aware programming language

By now, I have covered the first two. It's time to explore what an accompanying programming language could look like. We've already created a foundation for this with the query language presented earlier. By extending this with such concepts as functions, variables, and control flow, we can mold this into a general-purpose language. The result is a language that, by definition, doesn't suffer from any impedance mismatch with the underlying database, as it is completely integrated with that database.

To start this chapter on a sound footing, we begin with a number of concrete examples as to what these aforementioned language constructs might look like. Do realize, however, that this book is not intended to be a

© Jos Jong 2019
J. Jong, *Vertically Integrated Architectures,*
https://doi.org/10.1007/978-1-4842-4252-0_9

formal and detailed specification. First, because that would require a book of its own, but especially because an exact specification ought to be the result of an actual (reference) implementation.

Much more important than the exact syntax of the language are answers to questions such as the following:

- What is the position of that programming language in relation to implicit services and the database?

- How far can we go with the integration between all those concepts?

- What is the role of internal memory in a persistence-aware programming language?

- How do we deal with transactions?

- And, above all, how do we ensure the performance and scalability of this far-reaching form of integration?

The latter is, of course, one of the most fundamental questions. And it is not just the integration itself that helps in this respect. In this chapter, you will see that there is additional gain to be had by what in functional programming is called *pure functions*. A strict distinction between reads and writes massively contributes to the possibilities for optimization, directly and indirectly.

This approach does have an impact on the way source code is translated into executable code. It will be different from what we are used to with traditional compilers and interpreters. This also influences the way we store source code. In addition is the question of what the role of internal memory is when everything is built around persistence. I'll cover all of these topics.

But, as said, let's start with a few concrete examples, to show how we can extend the query language to a general-purpose programming language.

# Introducing Functions

The first step toward a general-purpose programming language is
providing the ability to define functions. Because the IR model is
effectively a variant of an object model, we can view every function as a
member function of an item or value type. This means that every function
invocation is provided with an implicit parameter that refers to the
corresponding item or value (the this or self parameter).

Let's start with the earlier customer/orders example. Considering the
ownership hierarchy, we could write it down like so:

```
database
    customer`s as subitems
        order`s as subitems
            line`s as subitems
                product as association to database product
                count as integer
    product`s as subitems
        name as text
        price as number
```

- As before, this is not intended to be a formal data
  definition language (DDL), but just a way to represent
  the examples in this book.

- The indentation here represents the property structure:
  customer and product are direct properties (subitems)
  of the database, order is a subitem of customer, and
  line is a subitem of order.

- as is used to denote the type of a property.

- association to indicates a unidirectional association between line and product.

- The xxx`s notation is a way to denote both the singular and the plural name. An alternative notation could be xxx\xxxs.

We can now define functions on every level in this data model. For example, to calculate the amount of an order line:

```
database
    customer`s as subitems
        order`s as subitems
            line`s as subitems
                product as association to database product
                count as integer
                function amount`s() returning number:
                    = count * product price
    product`s as subitems
        name as text
        price as number
```

- Just as with properties, it may be convenient, although not mandatory, to define both a singular and a plural name; hence the use of `s in the function name. You will see how this comes in handy in queries.

- The keyword returning specifies the result type of the function, though in many cases, this may be deduced from the body of the function, using type inference.

- As we specified this function as a member of item type line, we can directly access its properties count and product.

Given this function, we can now write queries such as this:

```
order-x lines amounts sum
```

- The result of this expression is the total amount of the order referred to by order-x.

- We are invoking the function amounts() here without parentheses because, from the perspective of the query, it is nothing more than a read-only property.

- We are using the plural name of the function amount`s, because an order may have multiple lines and, thus, the result of order-x lines amounts is also multi-valued (a set of number values).

Naturally, we can put this expression in a function of its own. At the level of order, we can define the following function:

```
database
    customer`s as subitems
        order`s as subitems
            line`s as subitems
                product as association to database product
                count as integer
                function amount`s () returning number:
                    = count * product price
            function total-amount`s () returning number:
                = lines amounts sum
    product`s as subitems
        name as text
        price as number
```

Functions may have parameters, of course, as in this example (at the level of order):

```
database
    customer`s as subitems
        order`s as subitems
            ...
            function discount`s(percentage as number)
                returning number:
                = total-amount * percentage / 100
```

We then can use this to determine what a discount of 3% would cost us, if we applied this to all orders of 10,000 or more:

```
customers orders [ total-amount >= 10000 ] discounts(3) sum
```

While these are relatively simple examples, they do show how business logic deriving data from other data can be built upon functions invoking each other—functions that we can then refer to from an implicit service call.

As sets are first-class citizens within the IR model and query language, we can even define functions on the level of a set. The functions count and sum are examples of this. They do not operate on individual objects but, rather, on a set of objects, in the case of count, on any arbitrary set, and for sum, on a set of number values. Although these are examples of natively implemented functions, so-called intrinsics, we may also define our own set-level functions, and not just on the level of values, but also for specific item types. Suppose we want to create a pie chart showing how the revenue is distributed among a set of customers. We can then define a set-level function on the level of customers (plural):

```
set-function turnover-percentages():
    = the customers {
        #(
            the customer,
```

```
        100 * orders total-amounts sum /
            the customers orders total-amounts sum
    )
}
```

- This function returns a set of (group-by) values containing both a reference to a customer and a percentage, just as with the result of a GROUP BY in SQL.

- The #(...) notation constructs the value (group-by) record, in this case, per customer.

- With the <type-reference>, we refer to a certain object of set in the context of an expression. Consider it to be an extended version of this or self. In this case, the customers refers to the set of customers on which the function is invoked.

- The {...} is a map function that goes through each of the customers and, because of #(...), creates a group-by value per customer.

- the customer within the {...} map fragment refers to the current customer during the execution of the map operation.

- For the sake of simplicity, I have omitted the return type here. But we could describe it as a set of #(customer, number).

Now suppose we want to create a pie chart for a given set of customers, referenced by the variable selected-customers. For this, we can use the following expression as a starting point:

selected-customers turnover-percentages

# About Variables

Variables can be useful to break up longer expressions, as in this example:

```
function foo() returning persons:
    var elder-persons = persons [ age >= 65 ]
    = elder-persons [ address city = 'London' ]
```

- The = here functions as a `return` statement.

In this chapter, we assume that variables can change value. Whether we should allow that is a matter of preference. There is nothing wrong with a more functional style, in which values can only be used as one-time assignable symbols, but it is important to realize that repeated assignment of values to a variable does not make a function less pure. In functional programming, a function is regarded pure if it has no side effects. And while the principle of one-time bindings is a very neat functional style, a second assignment to a variable is not a side effect in and of itself. In a persistence-aware programming language, we can say that a function is only unpure if a subsequent invocation, given the same state of the database, returns a different result.

In the preceding example, when filtering the `elder-persons`, we have direct access to the property `address` of `persons`. This is an advantage again of a set-oriented language, in which a set is not an instance of a generic collection class but an actual plural variant of the concerning type. As with any other expression, this can all be regarded as type- and cardinality-safe. The benefits of such a *static* approach compared to a dynamic approach is that the compiler actually knows which property of the given object we can access. That's good for such things as the execution optimizations, version management, code completion, and refactoring.

To help with this cardinality safety, we can optionally specify a singular and plural name for a variable, just as with elements in the database. Suppose we gather a set of customers and then want to select one by name, and name is defined as a unique attribute in the data model. We may then write

```
var customer`s = get-some-customers()
= customer [ name = 'Johnsson' ]
```

By using the singular form in the last line, we tell the compiler that we expect to return a single customer.

# Control Flow and Subcontexts

A control flow construct such as if-then-else could be devised as follows:

```
function foo() returning number:
    if has children [ age >= 18 ]:
        = children ages average
    else:
        = none
```

In case someone has at least one child age 18 or older, this function returns the average age of all children, otherwise, the value none (null).

A similar notation is feasible for a while. Although an if and while in this form follow an imperative nonfunctional style, we can still use them to implement pure functions. As mentioned, that's important for query optimizations. Enforcing a functional style (e.g., using recursion as an alternative to while) in that sense is only a matter of preference, not an essential choice.

Incidentally, no matter how useful a `while` may be here and there, in practice, a good for each construct is much more important. We have already showcased this a number of times using this format:

```
<set-expression>:
    <body>
```

As in this example:

```
var years = 0
employees [ age > 40 ]:
    years = years + years-of-experience
= years
```

- This totals the years of experience of all `employees` older than 40.

- `years-of-experience` in this example is assumed to be a property of the item type `employee`.

- We could have written this code without the use of a variable. `year` was deliberately added for the purpose of this example.

Within a `foreach` you have to be able to refer to the current object—the current employee, in the preceding example. That's why many programming languages have an explicit way of specifying a loop variable for that. For instance, like so:

```
foreach employee in employees:
    ...
    // note: other language
```

We can, however, do without such a variable. Already while discussing implicit services, we have seen how a `foreach` can be seen as creating a subcontext. This means we can directly access the current object's properties, like `years-of-experience`, in the preceding example. Think of this as a cross-breeding of a with statement (VB, C#, JavaScript, and other languages) and a localized this (self). And it is no different from what we have been doing in filters, such as with age > 40. By viewing this type of iteration context as a temporarily subcontext, we can write type-safe code without naming the iteration variable. This means there is no need to write something along this line:

```
// incorrect code
var years = 0
foreach employee in employees [ employee age > 40 ]:
    years = years + employee years-of-experience
= years
// end incorrect code
```

We could employ the following rules:

- Within the body of a function or procedure (methods that update data, discussed later), the initial context is the item, value, or set on which the method is invoked.

- Every filter, map, foreach, or similar construct creates a subcontext.

- To avoid confusion, you may only refer to properties of the current object, being the current context.

- If, with nested contexts, we want to refer to a context higher up in the hierarchy, we use the keyword the, followed by the name of the type or variable corresponding to that context.

Example:

```
customers:
    orders:
        if total-amount > the customer credit-limit
            ...
```

- total-amount in this case is a property of order, and within the subcontext of orders, we may refer to it directly.

- the customer enables us to refer to the parent context and thus the credit-limit property of the current customer.

We're once again helped by the fact that the IR model knows the singular and plural name of every type. This makes it possible to use customer to refer to the current object in the customers iteration.

Another example follows, now using filters:

```
employees [ has manager [ salary < the employee salary ]]
```

The exact syntax and details of the solutions sketched here are, of course, not the heart of the matter. There is no accounting for taste. What does matter, however, is that with such an approach, these language constructs become first-class citizens. That is the key to enabling us to optimize them way further than would be possible, using indirect ways like with explicit map(), filter(), and foreach() functions and closures.

# Procedures vs. Functions

As mentioned before, to strictly separate read actions from write actions, it makes sense to distinguish between functions and procedures. Functions can then by definition be 100% *pure*. And we can be very strict about only procedures being allowed to change the state of the system, just as with the distinction between functions and stored procedures in some SQL dialects, however, more modern, object-based, and stricter.

A procedure might look like this (defined as a member of `customer`):

```
procedure update-credit-limit(factor as number):
    if orders amounts sum >
            customers { orders amounts sum } average:
        credit-limit = 100000 * factor
    else:
        credit-limit = 10000 * factor
```

Procedures may both read and change data and may invoke both functions as well as other procedures. Functions are only allowed to read data and invoke other functions.

An implicit read service request, to a degree, is an anonymous function (or, rather, a tree of anonymous functions, because of its hierarchical capabilities). An implicit write service call can be seen as an anonymous procedure.

Most 3GLs do not distinguish between functions and procedures. To prevent unintended data changes further, they introduced constructs, such as immutable data, const, final, etc. In a persistence-aware language, we may resort to principles we already know from the database world, such as repeatable reads and transactions. Looking at reading and writing data in this more general way, the difference between functions and procedures becomes more natural and leads to more opportunities for optimizations. Procedures may only be invoked from within the context of a write-transaction that is logically bounded by an implicit service write request.

The distinction between functions and procedures also makes it easier to differentiate how to deal with exceptions. If something goes wrong while querying data (e.g., external system offline, division by zero, or whatever other reason), it is not required to let the complete service request fail. We can instrument the runtime in such a way that return values may include an error state. Functions receiving such an error value as input can automatically translate this into an error state in their own result. With the runtime being aware of this happening, it can still return all data that was not affected. As with authorization errors that we discussed before, think of this as a spreadsheet in which an error in a formula only makes dependent formulas fail, not the rest. On the other hand, a procedure that fails should always result in the rollback of the transaction at hand.

So much for this deliberation on how we can expand a set-oriented query language to become a persistence-aware programming language. As noted in the chapter's introduction, the big question is now how we can make this perform well.

# Making It Perform

Thus far, we have solved two potential performance bottlenecks that otherwise stand in the way of vertical integration. First, by achieving perfect granularity with implicit services, all intents of a client stemming from a single action (such as an update or screen refresh) can be bundled into a single network call. Given this, a client never has to break up its unit of work into multiple requests, completely eliminating the risk of any unwanted lazy loading issues and, therefore, any need to think about automatically preventing or optimizing this. Set aside that we no longer have to write code for standard read-write operations. In the next chapter, we shall see how this approach provides inroads for further integration, better reuse of client-side code, and for innovative solutions such as generic metadata-driven clients.

Second, by eliminating the distinction between application server and database, we get rid of the resulting impedance mismatch this introduced in the nineties. This allows for client requests to be directly translated into actual reads and writes against the database. As with perfect granularity, this means we also get rid of unintended lazy loading risks at this level. And as a result, we don't have to account for this in the business logic we write, which improves reusability.

What is left to discuss is how references to persistent data from the code we write can be translated into physical disk I/O actions. This third and final hurdle is the topic of the remainder of this chapter.

Implicit service requests ultimately lead to reading or modifying data that exists on a physical storage medium, whether it is a hard disk, SSD, or network attached storage. This seems like a straightforward problem. In theory, one could translate every read access to an item, relationship, or attribute into a read action for the corresponding bytes from storage. However, there are a number of pitfalls we need to avoid.

    a.   In order to locate specific data in relatively large databases, we cannot abstain from employing indexes in some shape or form.

    b.   While with an eye on reusability and maintainability we would like to construct business logic from singular functions and procedures, this may lead to huge inefficiencies, owing to the same data being retrieved or recalculated far too often.

    c.   If the combination of compiler and runtime are effectively not able to derive the intentions of the programmer from the source code, the potential for the optimization of the execution of that code is very limited.

Let's go into each of these points in detail.

Concerning indexes, point (a), it is obviously preferred that the compiler and runtime automatically figure out where and when an index is useful to solve a query, but this is not just for nicety. Leaving this to the programmer, as with some NoSQL and object databases, has a lot of major drawbacks.

- It means that we author the source code dependent on the fact of whether an index is or isn't available for a certain attribute or combination of attributes. That, among other things, means that fine-tuning the database performance can sometimes result in having to modify source code.

- It assumes the programmer knows best as to what access strategy (indexes) to utilize for a certain query. And that remains to be seen. The best access path can be different, depending on the context and the data statistics and may, therefore, change over time.

- It makes business logic less reusable, as you cannot always know beforehand whether and how service requests will combine the logic you write. An initially logical guess as to which indexes to use might have an adverse effect on retrospect.

In this respect, we can, of course, learn from RDBMS and other databases in which a programmer only writes down his/her intentions, after which an optimizer, supported by statistics of the actual data, decides on the (probably) best access path.

Point (b) is best explained with an example. Suppose we define this function on the item type person:

```
function older-than-average() returning boolean:
    = age > the database persons ages average
```

We can now ask any person whether he or she is older than the average age of all persons in the database.

```
person-x older-than-average
```

Given this function, let's determine which persons are older than average.

```
persons [ older-than-average ]
```

Suppose we have a database of 100,000 persons, and the compiler and runtime literally execute what the query and function say. That would lead to the expression the database persons ages average being executed 100,000 times. And that is 99,999 times too many, as we may assume that the average age will not change during the execution of the query (owing to repeatable reads and pure functional behavior).

While this is a simple example, it requires the caller of the older-than-average() function to know the consequences of its use, thus being aware of its implementation. But that contradicts with the desire to separate interface and implementation, let alone that the function we deal with gets more complex and nested deeply.

We could manually rewrite this business logic in such a way that the average is only calculated once, for example, by having to supply the pre-calculated average as a parameter to older-than-average(). But that undermines the self-containment and reusability of the individual parts of this setup.

Another option would be to have the database maintaining a cache and having it recognize that the result of persons ages average has been computed before. This is what some functional programming languages do in the form of memoization, often in the slipstream of lazy evaluation. But again, there is much to be learned from RDBMS. SQL optimizers can detect the dependencies between the individual parts of a query and use that knowledge to prevent unnecessary repeated execution.

Point (c) is concerned with the extent to which the compiler and runtime are able to understand the intention of a piece of source code. No matter what, this is a necessary condition to be able to automatically utilize indexes (point a) and prevent unnecessary repeated execution (point b). But it is a much broader subject, especially when persistent data is involved. Let's see why that makes such a difference.

# Beyond the von Neumann Model

As reiterated several times, on all fronts, there are things to be learned from existing database techniques. It all starts by distancing ourselves from the way we traditionally look at source code. In a 3GL, in whatever shape or form, the code we write is eventually translated into memory operations. The model this is based on is known as the von Neumann model (see Figure 9-1).

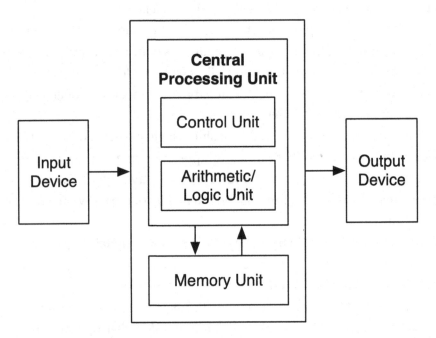

***Figure 9-1.***  *The von Neumann model/architecture*

Although the von Neumann model does not state whether the Memory Unit is concerned with persistent memory, in practice, it is always implemented as a computer's internal volatile memory It may be partly for that reason that in practically all programming languages, dealing with persistent data is seen as a separate concern, dealt with via I/O API operations. All this, despite the fact that, in the end, persistent data is the only way to represent a system's state, simply because electrical power is not a permanent thing. In this respect, internal memory is just there for intermediate results and to cache data for performance reasons. Maybe it is because the von Neumann model dates to a period in which batch-like processing was the only way to go.

A kind of trivial way to make data persistence a first-class citizen in programming languages is not to distinguish between internal and external memory at all. This division is not as fundamental as it may seem. It just happened to be there for historical reasons, because no memory technology was ever both persistent and fast at the same time. This might actually change in the future, with technologies such as Intel's 3D XPoint memory, who knows? It would alleviate things greatly. However, this does not address every concern.

Even when the physical access to data storage is extremely fast, we still don't want to spend I/O bandwidth and CPU cycles on unnecessary or just inefficient query execution. I've already mentioned the solution a few times before: a runtime optimizer. Both the IR model and the language sketched so far are conceptual enough to stay away from any specific execution plan. This gives an optimizer the freedom to completely turn the code you write inside out and upside down, whatever performs the best in a certain context. Be aware that this goes beyond typical compiler optimizations. 3GL compilers are only concerned with the optimization of low-level CPU instructions and memory operations. Although some functional programming languages go a step further with such things as lazy evaluation and memoization, even those never bother about using an index, depending on data statistics, or selectively skipping some pieces of code given a specific service request.

To apply such a mechanism to a fully-fledged programming language, there are a few hurdles to clear. We shall see shortly, however, that we can overcome all of them.

# Exploiting Referential Transparency

Probably one of the most impactful things we can do to optimize is to exploit the so-called *referential transparency* of pure functions. Referential transparency means that we can substitute any invocation of a function with the implementation of that same function, without any consequences for the outcome of the code at hand. This is only possible if the functions we deal with are 100% pure (i.e., idempotent and without side effects). That is, however, exactly what we achieved by strictly distinguishing between procedures and functions.

Function substitution is an essential step toward optimization, because it means an optimizer can perform a global analysis over all code involved. This is because it no longer has to take a reference to a function as a literal call to a separate method. Instead of optimizing each function separately, it can regard them as nested pieces of code that can be analyzed as one big tree of expressions. This allows the programmer to utilize the concept of functions as broadly as he/she wants, constructing business logic out of individually reusable components (functions), without any consequences for the runtime performance of that code.

Let's start with an example similar to the earlier average age problem. We can define this function for the item type customer, as follows:

```
function is-above-average-customer returning boolean:
   = turnover > the database customers turnovers average
```

which only returns true for customers who ordered more than the average turnover per customer. Suppose we then use this function with an additional condition about the region customers should be in.

```
customers [ is-above-average-customer and region = 4 ]
```

We can construct the compiler and runtime in such a way that this query, utilizing referential transparency, is internally rewritten as

```
customers [ turnover >
    the database customers turnovers average
    and region = 4 ]
```

Suppose turnover is itself a function on the level of customer.

```
function turnover`s returning number:
    = orders amounts sum
```

We can rewrite the query even further.

```
customers [ orders amounts sum >
    the database customers { orders amounts sum } average
    and region = 4 ]
```

- The map-operation using {...} is required in this case, to first determine the sum per customer, then the average.

If we repeatedly and consistently apply this rewriting to all queries within an implicit service call, we reduce them into their basic building blocks:

- References to the actually persisted properties of the model (so without intermittent functions calls)

- Mathematical and logical operations

- Filters, maps, and foreach operations

- Control flow statements

This is what we can use as input for the query optimizer, to determine an access strategy with the lowest cost, usually expressed in terms of the least amount of physical I/O.

Let's say the database has an index on the `customer` region field, and we are dealing with tens of thousands of `customers` and a few dozen regions. It stands to reason, then, that the optimizer decides to first find the keys of the `customers` in region 4 and only then calculate the outcome of `orders amounts sum` per `customer`. Otherwise, it would needlessly calculate the turnover for customers who are not relevant to the result.

A second optimization is one I've already discussed with the example of average `ages`. It is not necessary to compute the expression

```
customers { orders amounts sum } average
```

per `customer`, because there is no dependency on a specific customer. So, it suffices to compute this value once, and then compare it to the outcome of orders amounts sum for the customer at hand.

These are just a few examples, but we can go at least as far as any decent database engine will go. In addition to this, queries will often stem from an implicit service request. We can, therefore, take this optimization strategy one step further and have the service call analyzed as a whole. This can result in additional benefits, for example, in case there is overlap (similar expressions) in different parts of that request.

An optimizer, of course, changes the role of the compiler and runtime environment. It also has consequences for how we handle code from others, in the sense of libraries and their kin. That is a subject in and of itself, which I will delve into shortly. But first, I'll discuss the importance of intrinsics and set orientation.

# The Importance of Intrinsics

To enable a query optimizer to do all the suggested smart tricks, we need more than just referential transparency. There are a few other language constructs that the compiler must recognize, because they are relevant to determining an efficient access path to the physical data. Although with a slightly different purpose than with 3GLs, we know this concept as so-called compiler intrinsics.

Compiler intrinsics are language constructs that a compiler can decide to directly translate into low-level machine code, instead of a much slower function call. Most operators, such as >, =, and, and or, are typically intrinsics, because they can certainly be translated into very efficient code. It makes no sense to have them implemented as explicit function calls. But even things that look like real function calls can be bypassed in this way. A call to a function sin() could be translated into a hardware instruction for the floating-point processor. And a length() function for strings could be just one or two machine instructions. So that is a good candidate too.

In our persistence-aware language, we certainly want all these kinds of intrinsics, but we can stretch the concept into also recognizing things relevant for accessing persistent data.

An example:

```
person [ id = 123 ]
```

We want the compiler to recognize this comparison between id and 123, because it may be beneficial to translate this into an index lookup.

A function such as count() should also be recognized as intrinsic. Take this example:

```
customers [ region = 4 ] orders count
```

A naive implementation of the set-function count() would probably read all orders and then count them in memory. But as with an SQL COUNT(*), there are way better performing strategies to achieve the same result. If the relationship between customers and orders is stored as a physical array per customer, we can simply add the sizes of all those arrays. And if instead there is a foreign key referencing the customer from each order, we could probably use the index on that foreign key. So, even then, we never have to physically access the actual order records.

We can go quite far with this kind of intrinsics. For example, say that a function performs a sort(), but due to the way some business logic is combined, the order does not actually play a role in the end result, the sort operation could then be ignored.

On the other hand, it is certainly not necessary for all operations the language offers to be treated this way. It's fine to implement most of them as regular functions, be it in the language itself, so that referential transparency can do its job, or if that is beneficiary, in a native C or C++ implementation. What matters is to identify precisely those functions and language constructs that influence what physical access paths would be best when retrieving the data.

Some other examples:

- Operators such as and and or may sometimes better be translated to sets of keys, which can then be joined or intersected.

- For qualitative operators such as all, any, and has, it may suffice to detect only a single element, just as EXISTS() and NOT EXISTS() in SQL would do.

# The Contribution of Set Orientation

Besides the fact that set orientation, as introduced in Chapters 5 and 6, leads to a compact and elegant notation for queries, it also directly contributes to the optimization of program code. This is why we must pay attention to it here.

One of the main optimizations we can ensure with sets is that we do not always have to retrieve the actual underling objects. A property chain, for example, might mostly be implemented as a lookup of keys, just as with a set of joins in SQL.

Another advantage of a set-oriented programming language is that the compiler and runtime may parallelize the execution, where possible and beneficial. Take the following query:

```
customers [ region = 4 ] orders lines
```

Because with disk I/O we have to take into account a minimal latency per I/O request, when accessing bigger amounts of individual records, it essential, therefore, to fire as much I/O requests at once. After, they can be handled asynchronously. Synchronously waiting for the answer to one request before making the next can easily result in unacceptable response times and completely underusing the system's resources. The new NVMe standard does not have a queue depth of 64K per request queue for no reason. Depending on the need, a runtime may even put multiple threads to work, and as with reactive programming, we can even have multiple steps in a property chain being processed like an asynchronous stream of map operations.

# Source Code Reconsidered

The idea of a query optimizer requires us to rethink the way we typically deal with source code. Full pre-compilation into executable (virtual) machine instructions leaves no room for a runtime optimizer to analyze the code and makes it too late into the cycle to change the execution plan. We can only fully optimize a service request when we take into account all the relevant factors, including

- The specific expressions used in that request

- The data statistics

- The availability of certain indexes

All these factors require a runtime approach. That's why full-on compilation is not an option at all. One potential solution is to keep only source files and reinterpret these again and again for each service request. But that's not ideal either.

The biggest problem with source files is that they very much limit the options for any advanced form of version management, especially if we want to relate the versioning of source code with the evolution of the underlying data model. Traditional version management, such as with Git, is purely based on the comparison of two versions of a text file. While this works very well to systematically keep track of all changes made, it makes it impossible to establish a link between code modifications, data model changes, and corresponding migration mappings.

We need something that is kind of in between source code and executable code. Before presenting a solution, let's first dissect the code we write into these three categories:

1.  The definition of the data model (items, relationships, and attributes)

2.  The signatures of methods (functions and procedures)

3.  The bodies (implementations) of functions and procedures

Although we could use a DDL for the definition of the data model (category 1), there are very good reasons not to go with this approach. Only by storing these data definitions as data itself, metadata, as we tend to call this, can we highly integrate the versioning of the data model with automatic or semiautomatic migrations (i.e., schema mappings, as described earlier). Anyone who has worked with SQL DDL knows that on the one hand, a DDL can be a good thing to quickly reinstantiate a schema, but on the other hand, it can be a nightmare to keep in sync with the actual schema in the database. This is because both are totally disconnected, something we should prevent replicating.

200

How about category 2, the signatures of functions and procedures? In theory, we could just rely on DDL-like text files again, but the dilemmas here are exactly the same as with the data model itself. After all, the signatures of methods can be regarded as part of the data model, in the sense that both data structures and method signatures together represent the API the system exposes to the outside world. For that reason, we might have to support older versions of a signature to support older clients, as in the case of a schema migration. This is what distinguishes the signature from the body of a method. Clients, and even other code, can depend on the signature, but with an implementation, it is the other way around. It's dependent on the data model and other method signatures, but no code is directly dependent on another method's implementation. To conclude, it makes a lot of sense to deal with signatures in the same way as the rest of the data model: inside the meta model and no longer in the form of totally disconnected text files.

This leaves us with the method implementations—category 3—themselves. It would certainly be possible to keep them as text fragments and still work out a feasible way to combine this with the integrated version management of the meta model; however, other aspects of the source code then come into play.

It is not without reason that most IDEs keep a more or less pre-translated version of source code in a so-called abstract syntax tree (AST). It might all happen behind the scenes, but whether it is to perform syntax highlighting, code completion, code navigation, or refactoring, all these functions typically utilize the AST, because maintaining such an AST is way more efficient than scanning the same code again and again.

The interesting thing about ASTs is that they are also the perfect input for a query optimizer. That's because they can contain the original intent of the source code but still have a form in which it is way more efficient to analyze the code and all its internal and external dependencies.

The essence of an AST is that it regards code as data. If we combine that with the metadata describing the data model and the data describing signatures, we can build a meta-database, in which we put everything together. This sounds like quite a challenge but remember that the IR model helps us by not trying to force everything into tables with foreign keys. It can even be a good incentive to make the IR model more functional complete and efficiently implemented. This even extends to the integrated version control that can be useful for both application data and metadata.

With an AST as *intermediate language,* the code is processed in two stages (see Figure 9-2). The first stage parses source code into the AST, and the second stage uses the AST to generate executable (most likely virtual) machine code. The existing terms *interpreter* and *compiler* actually fit these two stages perfectly, as long as we accept that they deviate somewhat from their regular meaning. The first state is just interpreting (parsing) the code, to make sure it makes sense and fits the existing AST and metadata. The second stage is to combine (compiling) the pieces required from the AST to generate the executable code needed to execute a given service request. The interpreter is triggered when the developer adds changes to the source code. The compiler is only triggered when a service request comes in. Any optimizations occur in the compiler.

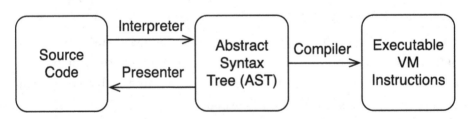

***Figure 9-2.*** *Abstract syntax tree as single truth*

With this approach, it may be tempting to keep a copy of every piece of source code that is interpreted and merged into the AST. We could, however, also regenerate the source code from the AST, by a process that basically does the exact opposite of the interpreter, called the *presenter* in Figure 9-2. There are very good reasons to do so.

- It simplifies things, by having a single copy of everything, a so-called single source of truth (SSOT).

- It allows for certain types of refactoring, without even having to change all related code. (See following.)

- It means that the method implementation can benefit from the integrated version management that we require anyway, without the need of a complex way to also keep the pieces of source code in sync with these versions.

The trick is to accommodate the AST, so that it can store visual source code elements such as line spacing and comments. We must be able to find a balance in this respect between a kind of enforced coding style, which could be a blessing for a lot of teams, and some freedom to lay out the code in the way we like. The presenter can use this to re-create the close-to-original source code, while the compiler can just ignore all these details.

The way this strategy helps with refactoring lies in the fact that the AST can directly reference elements in the meta model, using internal keys, not names. Therefore, changing the name of a data element of the method would not require an update of any code. It's like having a single source of truth at this level. The biggest risk with this might be conflicting names in existing method implementations. There are, however, ways to overcome this, such as implicitly translating local names (a variable or parameter) with a different name (e.g., x~2 instead of x) to keep them separate, or by using the keyword the to make sure a certain object and not a local variable is referenced. An application developer can still fix the name, but she or he doesn't have to do this immediately. This makes naming conflicts a local issue and no longer a hurdle to make such global changes as renaming an attribute in the data model.

With an AST, files, although greatly beneficial with contemporary tool sets, would be completely extraneous, and source code could be navigated with the data model as outline. This is very similar to Smalltalk, in which you navigate through packages, classes, methods, and code through a System Browser (see Figure 9-3).

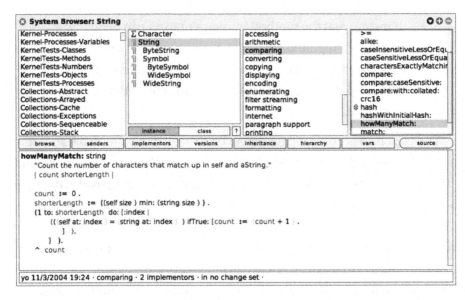

***Figure 9-3.*** *Example of a Smalltalk System Browser (Squeak)*

The idea of storing source code as data is not entirely new. Elements of it cannot only be found in Smalltalk but also, more recently, in something like Microsoft Language Server (`https://langserver.org/`). All have varying degrees of success, of course, but especially because of the goal of supporting different versions of a model, we should at least look at this again.

So much for the interpretation and presentation of source code. It is important to understand the separation between interpreting and compiling as not just being two stages. It is also completely decoupled from the unit of work these two stages work on. The interpreter only comes to life when a developer changes a piece of code, and only then does it interpret that specific piece of code. The compiler, however, gathers everything required for a given services request across the whole AST and data model.

It is also important to see that it is not necessary to compile the same type of client request over and over again. The compiler can maintain a cache to reuse executing plans, as long as the related AST and data model are not changed (both are a matter of dependency scanning to invalidate this cache). The cache could also be cleared when other parameters change, for example, when an index is added or changed. Although a service request does not require the concept of parameters per se, the compiler can very easily recognize all the constants in a request and, therefore, see that it can reuse an earlier plan just by replacing a few constants. This is what SQL prepared statements are all about. But as we can see, this can be detected automatically in many cases.

Again, we can gain so much knowledge related to all these things from existing database implementations. It is just that a persistence-aware programming language is stretching all these concepts.

Another point to be made here is that using an AST as input for the compiler inevitably means that we should also exchange code from third parties in the form of AST data. For individual helper functions, it may still suffice to receive them as pre-compiled VM code, but as soon as a persistent data model is involved, we want the compiler to have access to the AST of the associated methods. This does not, however, have to be a problem within an enterprise context or when open source policies are applied. If a given party really does not want to be that open, it could simply expose its data model, using implicit services.

The preceding exposition seems to be mostly about server-side code, but we can certainly involve the client side as well, provided it has its own code. But that is a topic that will be discussed in the next chapter.

# The Role of Internal Memory

All deliberations so far have been concerned only with the persistence awareness of the proposed language. But what about volatile data? In the background, the internal memory still plays a role. The question is, however, what role exactly?

To answer that question, we have to realize that the internal memory has always served two different roles:

1. To store intermediate results, typically implemented by way of a stack used to exchange parameters, local variables, and return values

2. A heap on which individual objects can be allocated, giving them a lifespan that exceeds the duration of function calls, unless otherwise arranged

Although technically different, these two roles get intermingled a lot. The reason for this lies in the fact that in many object-oriented languages, objects can only be created with so-called reference semantics. This means that even when value semantics, and, for that matter, the stack, would suffice, objects are still allocated on the heap, just for the purpose of their being an object. This then introduces the risk of unintentionally sharing the reference to that object beyond the scope of the code at hand, or even across threads, which makes it harder to force functions to always be pure functions. If they are not, it is harder to optimize their execution without additional tricks, such as classifying data as immutable, const, or final, or something like transactional memory. I have touched on this subject before, when discussing values vs. items.

The solution to this dilemma is to look at it in a much more conceptual way. Owing to the nested nature of functions, data in the form of parameters, local variables, intermediate results, and return values are a perfect to be handled on a stack. The fact that we still have to allocate some of the corresponding data on the heap is purely a historical and technical artifact. The main technical reason is typically that objects of variable size, such as collections and strings, don't behave very well on a stack. However, the fact that most object-oriented languages have no first-class support for value semantics also plays a big role.

Conceptually, the involvement of the heap for value semantics is of no consequence. If we look at it this way, we can completely hide this from the application developer. This is how some, mainly functional, programming languages deal with this. Although they use the heap as a technical extension to the stack, they do not expose this in the form of object references. This makes it easier to force functions to be pure and to prevent raise conditions when concurrency comes into play.

Given the idea of a query optimizer exploiting referential transparency, we can actually go one step further with this whole abstraction. We can give the optimizer the freedom to determine an access strategy that leaves little remains of the original imaginary (conceptual) stack. While the execution of the code will still employ a runtime stack, it no longer has to follow the original intent of the source code. In this way, parameters, local variables, and return values are just concepts to harness code complexity but not at all determinative of the actual execution.

In addition to this imaginary stack, purely dealing with value semantics, we do, of course, still use reference semantics with respect to the items in the database. Although, at first sight, this seems to contradict the idea of pure functions, it doesn't, because every call to a function in the database occurs within the context of a transaction. By designing read transactions to always deliver so-called consistent reads, every function can still behave fully idempotently. We could think of this as a form of transactional memory, but persistent rather than volatile. Again, we are just stretching the idea of a database into the realm of a general-purpose programming language.

With all this, the remaining question now is whether we still want to expose the idea of a heap to the application developer at all. In other words, must we still be able to allocate individual objects in volatile memory and subsequently refer to them using references? The answer is probably no.

First and foremost, unless managed by transactions, referring to shared volatile objects really does not go along with pure functions and, therefore, with all the optimizations discussed so far. But the question is also why we would require such in-memory objects at all? The distinction between internal and external memory is arbitrary anyway. As mentioned before, this emerged for technical and economic reasons. If we allow for the creation of objects in memory, we create a form of volatile system state. In 3GLs, we cannot do without, because it allows us to manage low-level things such as caching, transactions, or user sessions. But all of these are put in a completely different light within the concept of a persistence-aware programming environment in which we program in terms of the only state an information system can really have, which is a persistent state.

There are certainly exceptions to these rules, for example, to represent the state of a user interface. But in that case, it is all about the containment of the state. Also, on the server, we might want to keep certain user-level (session) related things that are volatile. However, as long as these types of data manipulations are transactional, we can give them a place in the runtime.

# Summary

I started this chapter by sketching what a persistence-aware programming language might look like. Not to figure out all the details, but to have a concrete starting point from which to consider how such a language might work in practice, especially how we can implement it as efficiently as possible, to allow the application developer to fully focus on the desired functionality. It has become apparent that we can draw a lot of inspiration from functional programming languages, not to strive for a purely functional style per se, but because we may utilize the referential transparency property of pure functions and related value semantics for full per-request optimizations.

Another prerequisite for this form of optimization is to identify certain language constructs as intrinsics, for example, to translate filter conditions into instructions to consult a database index.

Making collections first-class citizens by way of set orientation is yet another essential ingredient. It helps the interpreter and compiler to regard queries as specifications for data paths in the conceptual model, rather than a sequence of `map()` and `filter()` functions.

Finally, we have seen that for full per-request optimization the traditional ahead-translation of code into (virtual) machine instructions is of no use at all, and that keeping only source files as a single point of truth is far from ideal. By having an interpreter translate the source code into an AST, instead, we can better relate the version management of the code to the evolution of the underlying data model. A compiler can then use this AST to subsequently generate a per-request execution plan.

Of course, a programming language entails many more aspects than discussed in this chapter. But, as said, my goal here was only to determine the prerequisites for a persistence-aware programming language, in order to support us in the vertical integration of database and application logic.

I've intentionally kept the client's implementation out of the equation so far, because there are so many options for that—from those that are 100% integrated and generic to those having a completely free format and purely utilizing the implicit service interface. There are also a lot of specifics to account for when it comes to both user interfaces and external systems, enough, at least, to devote the entire last chapter of this book to this subject.

# CHAPTER 10

# User Interface Integration

*As far as the customer is concerned, the interface is the product.*

—Jef Raskin

Even the most obscure nonintegrated user interface (UI) client can benefit from the integration that we have achieved on the server so far. By making sure that implicit services can be expressed in a human readable JSON-over-HTTP format, the VIA architecture is open to any client, UI or not.

In addition, the *perfect granularity* of implicit services gives a client full control over the data streams to and from the back end. This means that as long as we stay within the defined data model, we can change screens as much as we like, without any need to modify server-side code. Given an implementation of the previously explained server-side schema version mapping, this still holds when a client does not catch up with the current data model version (within practical limits, of course). That's not just a technical advantage. It also means that developers are less dependent on one another, leading to higher productivity and more agile teams. However, we can stretch the idea of vertical integration way further than that.

Despite UIs being concerned with things other than the server, such as the visual aspects of presenting data and the related user interaction, everything that happens in the UI is still very much related to the data in the back end. In most screens, every field, row, column, tab, or other visual

J. Jong, *Vertically Integrated Architectures*,
https://doi.org/10.1007/978-1-4842-4252-0_10

element is directly bound to corresponding properties or functions in the data model. If not, it is probably because some client-specific logic is calculating or transforming server-side data in some way, still implying a relationship with the data model.

This will remind some people of so-called form-based development tools that many will regard as inflexible and domain-limited, certainly not general purpose. That's kind of true for a lot of SQL and traditional 4GL-based tools. This is partly the result of the focus on data entry and the business orientation of these tools. It is also a side effect of the underlying programming environment that is SQL-based or, at least, table-based, in most cases. The latest low-code development environments such as OutSystems and Mendix already prove how much further we can stretch the concept of data-model-bound screen definitions, in light of their relatively rich UI features, flexible layout, and custom UI controls.

The IR model and the idea of implicit services create even more opportunities in this direction. Their general-purpose object-model nature can bring us a lot of malleability and scalability. Think about reusable self-defined UI controls with the flexibility of any mature 3GL GUI-framework or deeply nested small-sized screen elements without unreasonable performance penalty. As with other form-based tools, the VIA architecture can also make sure that server-side data model constraints are automatically reused by, and executed within, the client.

To achieve all this, we have to rethink a few things about screen definitions and their relationship with the underlying data model. In this chapter, we will look into two major challenges in this respect:

- How we can automate the way screens retrieve data from the server in a scalable way

- How to deal with unsaved (uncommitted) data, with the purpose of local business logic such as the aforementioned constraints and other local data calculations in general

I will begin this chapter by discussing these two subjects. After that, I will cover the different kinds of implementations possible, in which I will also consider the massive opportunities offered by generic query tools and so-called *end-user development.*

# Query Aggregation

The concept of implicit services is not just eliminating the need to write explicit service implementations. It can also be highly beneficial with respect to building UIs. Let's see how something that we will call *query aggregation* can help us to apply typical programming concepts such as encapsulation, locality, and reuse to the world of screens, pixels, and user interaction.

With programming, we have learned to use classes, modules, and functions to manage complexity and enable code reuse. There are two reasons why it can be difficult to achieve the same kind of modularity with building screens.

The first obstacle is that with some UI frameworks, such things as layout, styling, and certain behaviors (e.g., form fields) are defined in such a way that it is difficult or impossible to isolate them into separate components. HTML, for example, has never been very flexible in this regard, because of its origin as a page-formatting language. Although new developments such as Web Components are trying to work around that, traditional 3GL GUI libraries always perform better in this area. With every widget, subview, window, or whatever it is called, being represented by an instance of a class, they typically make it easier to build self-contained UI components, both for custom-made generic controls and for domain-specific reusable screen components. In that sense, we already know how to solve this aspect of UI modularization.

However, this doesn't solve a second hurdle for modularization, which has everything to do with the UI being dependent on the underlying data model. Even with the best component-style GUI frameworks, there is no way around this. And this is where query aggregation comes in. Let's start with an example to illustrate the problem.

Let's say we create a screen to show some basic information for a customer, like that in Figure 10-1.

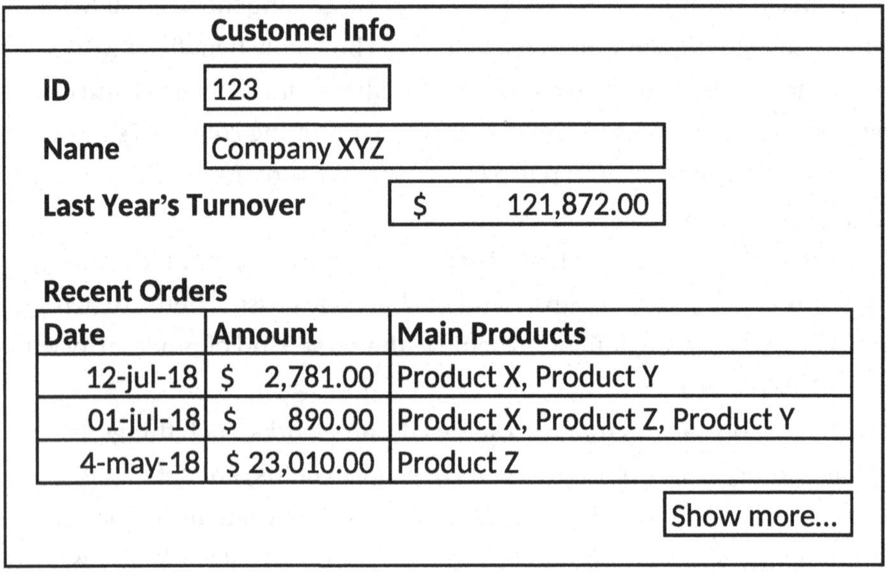

| Customer Info | | |
|---|---|---|
| **ID** | 123 | |
| **Name** | Company XYZ | |
| **Last Year's Turnover** | $          121,872.00 | |

**Recent Orders**

| Date | Amount | Main Products |
|---|---|---|
| 12-jul-18 | $   2,781.00 | Product X, Product Y |
| 01-jul-18 | $      890.00 | Product X, Product Z, Product Y |
| 4-may-18 | $ 23,010.00 | Product Z |

Show more...

***Figure 10-1.*** *Customer info screen*

Imagine that the implicit service request required to load the data for this screen from the back end is as follows:

```
company [ id = 123 ]:
    :: id
    :: name
    :: orders [ today – date <= duration(1, year) ]
            amounts sum
    orders sort(date, descending = true) first(5):
```

```
:: date
:: amount
:: lines sort(amounts) last(3) products
         names joined(', ')
```

This is obviously a simple example. But say we want both the recent orders table section (including the Show more... button) and the rows within that table to be self-contained as separate components (reusable subviews) in whatever form the given UI framework supports. In that case, writing the full-service request, as here, is a very page-oriented approach, contradicting with the idea of splitting the UI into self-contained components.

In theory, we could have individual screen components read their own pieces of data from the server, but that could potentially result in unacceptable performance, although not so much, if we are talking about a few separate sections within a screen. That would not be different from so-called *portlets* being fully self-contained and responsible for getting their own data. But for anything that iterates over sets of objects, such as each individual row in the example, this is a no-go.

Fortunately, we can have the UI runtime help us out in this respect. The idea of the aforementioned *query aggregation* is as follows:

- Every screen element can expose its local data needs to a central runtime component.

- This central component combines (aggregates) all these individual requests into a single server request whenever data is to be loaded.

This concept draws from the fact that with implicit services, we do not have to predefine an API for the screen in question, and an implicit service request can consist of any thinkable nested combination of queries and expressions. So, there is no need for a central runtime to know in advance what data to retrieve. It can just combine all the subviews' local requests.

Interestingly, these separate queries are never in complete isolation. Each of them happens within a certain object context. So, we can apply the persistence-aware programming language concepts such as set orientation and subcontext to this idea. To explore this, let's assume we have a specification language at our disposal to define the screen in Figure 10-1 with the proposed subsections (the recent orders section and, within that, order rows). The definition of the screen itself could then look like this:

```
screen customer-info-screen:
    context-type = customer
    title = 'Customer Info'
    number-field:
        title = 'ID'
        data-binding = id
    text-field:
        title = 'Name'
        data-binding = name
    number-field:
        title = 'Last Year''s Turnover'
        data-binding = orders [ today - date
            <= duration(1, year) ] amounts sum
        decimals = 2
        prefix = '$'
    sub-view:
        name = recent-orders-section  // defined below
        context = the customer        // parameter
```

We're ignoring any layout aspects here on purpose. The preceding language is just a kind of pseudo screen definition language to illustrate the idea of data model bindings.

The definition for the recent-orders-section and nested order-row subviews could look like this:

```
subview recent-orders-section:
    title = 'Recent Orders'
    context-type = customer    // type of incoming parameter
    table-view:
        data-binding = orders
            sort(date, descending = true) first(5)
        column-titles = ('Date', 'Amount',
            'Main Products')
        row-sub-views = order-row    // defined below
    button:
        title = 'Show more...'
        on-click = ...

subview order-row:
    type = table-row
    context-type = customer order
    date-field:
        data-binding = date
    number-field:
        data-binding = amount
        decimals = 2
        prefix = '$'
    text-field:
        data-binding = lines sort(amounts)
            last(3) products names joined(', ')
```

The essence of this example is in the context-type and data-binding clauses. The context-type for the customer-info-screen indicates that the screen is parameterized by a customer. This is like defining a customer-id parameter in the URL for a web page. However, because the whole idea

217

here is to integrate with the query language, we regard the customer item itself as the parameter. Think of it as a reference to a customer, although we are ignoring the technical details here, because it is all about the concepts.

Given the `context-type` being a customer, we can directly refer to properties of such a customer as `id`, `name`, or `orders`. In this sense, a screen or subview can be regarded as a subcontext in the same way we create a subcontext in the programming language by iterating over a set of objects.

The subview, named `recent-orders-section`, is passed on the customer with the statement `context = the customer`. So, even within the definition of the `recent-orders-section`, we can directly refer to properties of a customer, such as with the order's `sort(date, descending = true) first(5)` expression, which populates the table with the last five orders of the given customer. As said, this is a very simplified example, but it shows how subviews can be self-contained and still refer to the data model in its own subtext. That is what this is all about, without implying anything about how and when the concerning data must be loaded.

Iterating these orders results in (a maximum of) five subview instances named `order-row`, which themselves have the item type `order` as subcontext. This means that each `order-row` subview can directly refer to properties of its corresponding single order.

This is where query aggregation makes the most impact. Although these subviews seem to execute their own tiny queries, the client's runtime can combine all the subqueries to a single implicit service request, as shown at the beginning of this section. So, instead of loading each order with a separate query, the whole screen will be refreshed with a single network round-trip. It is not so much this query aggregation itself that counts here, but the fact that we can now mix and match reusable UI components at any level, without unreasonable performance penalties.

The runtime could be triggered to refresh the whole screen when a different customer is being assigned to the `customer-info-screen`, which then trickles down to reload every subview, therefore gathering all the subqueries from its subviews. But say we replace the `number 5 in` first(5) with a parameter and associate some source code with the Show more... button to increase that number. Clicking that button results in the need to refresh the table-view within the recent-orders-section subview, but there is no reason to refresh the whole screen.

We could achieve this selective behavior by the compiler or runtime analyzing the dependencies involved. They could determine that a change of the local parameter influences the orders query and, for that matter, the rows but not the rest of the screen. Imagine that clicking Show more... increases the parameter from 5 to 15. The resulting service request could then look like this:

```
company [ id = 123 ] orders
    sort(date, descending = true) first(15):
    :: date
    :: amount
    :: lines sort(amounts) last(3) products
               names joined(', ')
```

With the runtime assembling a specific request each time, depending on the actual data refresh needed, we get the best of two worlds. While making it possible to create self-contained and potentially reusable UI components, the coordinated approach makes sure that this still goes together with a single round-trip, with low latency as a result.

Putting database queries inside UI code is typically regarded as bad practice. However, we must understand why this is.

1. The mix of UI code and database code can introduce complexity that is better managed by keeping them separate.

2. Owing to query overhead and network latency, it can be a performance nightmare if each individual row or section in a screen fires its own database query.

3.  Directly binding a screen element to a database API
    makes it impossible to reuse them with in-memory
    (temporary or volatile data) scenarios.

The drawback of this separation is, however, having to write more code
and, therefore, in a way, introducing more complexity. The good news
here is that we can counter argument (1) with the clean and conceptual
approach of the query language proposed in this book. Issue (2) is solved
by the query aggregation just explained. In the next section, you will learn
how we can solve problem (3) with a transactional approach that supports
uncommitted data.

Query aggregation could be implemented as part of a generic fully
VIA-compliant client runtime that can execute screen definitions as in
the preceding examples. It is also quite possible for it to be supported by a
JavaScript web framework that gathers the individual expressions from a
hierarchy of UI components and then interacts with these components to
handle any refresh that may be needed.

The biggest challenge is in the level to which the client understands the
involved queries and expressions. A dumb approach could just combine
strings of sub-expressions. A client-side query engine, however, would
enable the client to understand things like dependencies on the client's
local state, such as the user expanding or collapsing items in a tree, or the
number of orders to load in the previous examples.

There are other reasons why a client-side query engine can be useful. I
will discuss these in the next section, about handling uncommitted data.

# Handling Uncommitted Data

Query aggregation is a perfect match for read-only screens, but as soon as
the user is allowed to change data, we must also deal with uncommitted
data—uncommitted in the sense of not yet being saved (committed) to

the server. That brings a whole different set of challenges than just reading data. Therefore, in the spirit of this book, in this section, we will investigate whether and how we can automate this *update* aspect of UIs too.

Obviously, just postponing a commit is as simple as gathering all the changes made by a user and creating an update request only after the user clicks a Save button. That's the easy part. The actual challenges are in how, when, and where to run business logic that we might want to execute on this uncommitted data. This is first and foremost relevant for executing constraints. Especially with more complex constraints, or ones that involve higher volumes of data, we are faced with the dilemma of processing them either on the server or on the client. Traditionally, we would solve this by design, but it is interesting to see how far we can stretch vertical integration to help us in this respect.

In addition to constraints, for some screens, we may also want to execute other calculations on uncommitted data. For example, we may want to calculate the total amount of the data we enter that is already updated before we save the data to the server, or determine the fact (i.e., a logical expression) of whether a certain part of the UI should be enabled, depending on other data that you enter. Because the challenge for these kinds of expressions are exactly the same as with constraints, we will focus on constraints for now. In a way, a constraint is just a special form of deriving data, in the sense that it always returns a logical value for which `false` means that the data is not compliant with the constraint defined.

Constraints have everything to do with uncommitted data, because we want a system to make sure that only data that complies to these constraints becomes publicly available. So, by definition, checking constraints occurs before saving any changed or new data. Executing a constraint on committed data should always return `true`.

In theory, a client could delegate all data validations to the server, but there is a very good reason why we want a UI client to perform the same checks up front: ergonomics. It is just so much nicer to be informed that a field is required, or to know that a given name is already in use, before you click Save, even though the end result is the same.

Constraints could be anything: checking whether a given property is filled (not empty), a name is not yet in use (uniqueness), or a given amount is not higher than that allowed by a given formula, to mention only a few examples. In theory, they can range from the simplest to massively complex expressions. And, as we will see, that influences the level of automation we can achieve.

Let's start with the simplest ones: constraints that say that some attributes are mandatory. Whether we're talking about a fully native generic forms-executing client engine or a JavaScript framework to help build free-format web forms, both could retrieve the relevant metadata from the server and use that to warn the user that a given field should be filled. They can even automatically show an icon (or *) to mark mandatory fields. In a way, this is just an extension to the idea of query aggregation, because metadata is still data that could be requested in the same service call that we use to fill the screen initially, as long, of course, as the query language has a way to access that metadata.

It might not sound like a big deal to have the client automatically figure out what fields are mandatory. We could certainly arrange this within the form itself. But it makes a lot of sense with a more universal form builder tool or in a generic query and data entry tool. Just as NOT NULL meta information is interpreted by generic SQL tools to indicate mandatory fields or columns.

We could do the same with checking the cardinality of relationships. Of course, typically, the difference between singular or plural also will be reflected in the design of the screen itself. But something such as checking whether we entered at least one order line while entering a new order is something we can implement in the same way as described previously for mandatory attributes.

So, for simple constraints, we could use the metadata from the data model. Now let's see what happens if we allow slightly more complex constraints.

Say we require the user to always enter a city when someone's e-mail address was entered. This involves multiple fields. In the data model, we could express this at the level of the city attribute, as follows:

```
not-empty or (empty and this person email empty)
```

If we can also associate a (multilingual) text with every constraint, a client could automatically show a message like

*City required when e-mail address is entered*

To validate a constraint such as this, we obviously require some sort of expression engine as part of the client runtime. That, of course, puts such a client or framework in a whole different league. However, if we can achieve this level of integration, we relieve ourselves of duplicating constraints on both the client and the server. It's another form of single point of truth, in which the UI automatically reflects all the constraints defined in the data model, with less code to write.

Following the idea of a pre-interpreted abstract syntax tree (as described in Chapter 9), the server can lower the burden for the client. It means that the constraints are already available in a close-to-executable way, with direct references to the meta model. So, depending on the level of integration, it might not be necessary for the client to parse any source code itself.

Clients that do not include their own execution engine could fall back to a mix of two strategies. They could still check for the relatively simple mandatory-or-not constraints and then relying on the server to do all other data validations when the user saves data. A generic mechanism to show any messages returned by the server completes the whole thing. These messages could even include internal references to the relevant data elements to neatly highlight the related fields.

Given a client-side execution engine, we can go a long way with automatically reusing constraints and other logic that works on uncommitted data. But there are still a few challenges.

In the e-mail/city example, we were assuming that both fields are on the same screen. If that's the case, the engine only has to understand the bindings between the fields and the model and use that to know on what fields to execute the logical expression. But what if a constraint partly involves data that is not entered on the same screen?

Let's illustrate this with an example (see Figure 10-2).

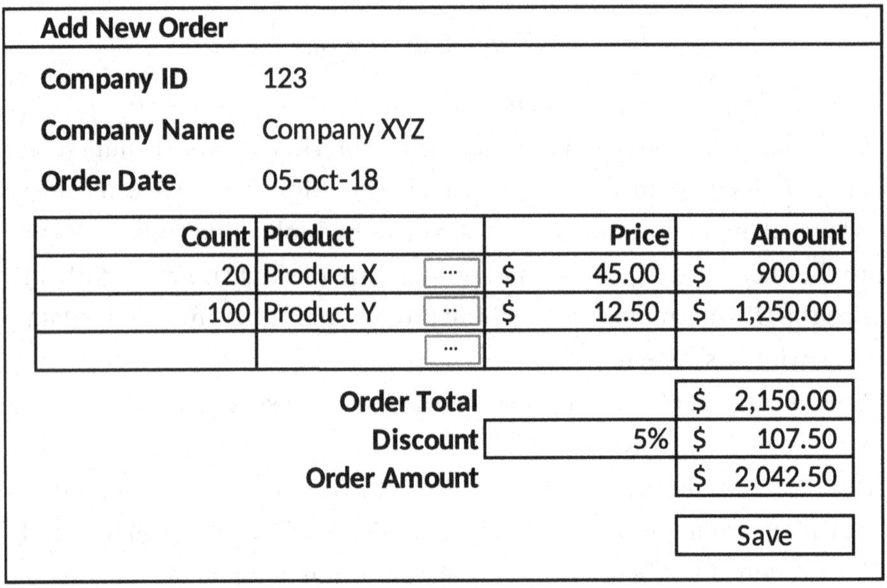

---

**Add New Order**

**Company ID**       123

**Company Name**   Company XYZ

**Order Date**       05-oct-18

| Count | Product | | Price | Amount |
|---|---|---|---|---|
| 20 | Product X | ... | $   45.00 | $   900.00 |
| 100 | Product Y | ... | $   12.50 | $ 1,250.00 |
| | | ... | | |

|  | | |
|---|---|---|
| Order Total | | $ 2,150.00 |
| Discount | 5% | $   107.50 |
| Order Amount | | $ 2,042.50 |
| | | Save |

---

***Figure 10-2.*** *Screen to add new orders*

The idea of this screen is that we can add an order for the earlier selected customer 123 by entering one or more order lines. The Save button will trigger a service request to create the order on the server. The only editable fields are count, product selection, and the discount percentage. The product price is automatically retrieved, and all the amounts are calculated based on expressions defined within the screen definition. I will not go into detail on how all this can be defined in such a language. We're only focused here on the challenges of constraints in the context of uncommitted data.

Imagine the following constraint:

> *For new customers, we're allowed only to enter orders with a maximum total of $5,000 (in the sense of a credit limit), until that customer is screened by a colleague.*

Let's say that we have an attribute `screened` within the `customer` item type that a colleague can set to `true` after due diligence, using a different screen. The preceding constraint can then be expressed as follows:

```
// within the context of 'customer'
= screened
  or lines amounts sum <= 5000

// note: assuming amount`s = product price * count
```

This is an example in which not all fields involved are mapped to the current screen. The solution is still relatively simple: in the process of aggregating a service request, the client runtime can include all the data elements it needs to execute the relevant constraints. So, apart from loading the customer id, name, and the order details (the last one assuming we can also edit existing orders), it only has to also request the customer screened value. This means that the single service request to load or refresh the screen also supplies this value.

Now say that the company wants to simplify its screening process. Instead of relying on a screening by another colleague, the new policy only requires a customer to at least have one earlier order that has been paid before he or she can order products worth more than $5,000. So, the constraint is changed to this:

```
= customer orders [ paid ] count > 0
  or lines amounts sum <= 5000
```

This is where we encounter a dilemma. The orders [ paid ] count > 0 expression results in a single true/false value. So, it makes sense to have the server execute that part, instead of the client loading all orders and then executing the expression within the client. In theory, it is possible to do it on the client, but if we have to load thousands or tens of thousands of items just to calculate a simple total or true/false value, a construct like this could result in unacceptable performance. The question now is how the client and server can figure out how to efficiently split such a task.

A potential solution is an automatic analysis of the dependencies within the expression. Any query or expression can eventually be represented as a tree of operations and suboperations. This means that on many occasions, a client or server is potentially able to understand which subtrees are dependent on uncommitted data and which ones are not. If we visualize the preceding example in an expression tree, we will see that the customer branch is not bound to anything that can change on the screen. The lines branch, however, does, because it is bound to the editable order lines table.

Achieving this level of automation would be great, of course. There is, however, one final challenge that is not easily covered by this kind of dependency analysis. That's when things are mixed up.

Let's say that the salesperson can negotiate any discount percentage he or she thinks is appropriate, but only within these bounds:

- A maximum of 5%, if the company ordered products worth less than $100,000 in the last year

- A maximum of 10%, if the company ordered products worth at least $100,000 in the previous year

We could formalize this into the following constraint:

```
var last-year-total =
    orders [ today - date <= period(1, year) ] amounts sum
if last-year-total >= 100000:
    = discount-percentage <= 10%
else:
    = discount-percentage <= 5%
```

At first sight, you might think that a dependency analysis of this expression (as discussed in the previous chapter, despite an imperative-style with a variable, this expression still qualifies as a pure functional lambda) could result in the last-year-total being calculated on the server and the rest calculated on the client. But does that make sense? The screen itself is also adding a new order. It is obviously a design decision whether the new orders should be included in the total. But it is a reasonable requirement. So, let's assume that. This means that the order path is at least partly dependent on uncommitted data.

Given a dependency analysis, this would mean that the whole constraint should be executed on the client. Unfortunately, this introduces two problems:

- First, it means that the dependency analysis has to understand the fact that the screen is adding a new order, meaning that orders should be interpreted as being the orders from the server plus the new one.

- Second, it means that the query aggregation will have to load all existing orders of the previous year. This might not be a problem in this case, but it could result in an unacceptable volume of data in other scenarios.

The first issue can be challenging, but it is probably easily solved. It is no different to what database servers do all the time when you update data during a transaction. For the duration of the transaction, servers create a sort of virtual data view that is a mix of the committed data overwritten with the data changes so far. In this way, they can simulate the effect of creates, updates, and deletes, even though not all data is committed yet. A fully vertically integrated client could do the same thing, by keeping track of every new or deleted item and every changed relationship or attribute.

The second issue is a more fundamental problem. Automatically figuring out the best strategy for such a scenario is not that obvious. The fact that the analysis process needs to know about the data volume is not even the biggest problem. This could be complex to implement, but it's kind of similar to what query optimizers have done for tens of years in database servers. The question is more how such an optimizer would be able to figure out the most sensible solution, for example, to total the amounts of existing orders on the server and then add the total amount of the new order on the client's side. This seems to go beyond the current query optimizer strategies, but it might be an interesting computer science subject to pursue.

To be practical, as long as we do not have a solution to this problem, we have at least three second-best alternatives.

1.  Making sure that the developer can disable the given server-side constraint to be reused in the client and, thus, accept that it will only be evaluated when data is saved to the server.

2.  A variant to this, in which the server allows a noncommitting save request. This means the client could try to save the data and see whether this returns any errors from the server. This can happen in the background, while the user is still entering data, triggered by certain kinds of changes made and maximized to a given number of calls per minute, let's say once every five seconds, at most.

3.   Finally, we could make it possible to overwrite a given server-side constraint in a way that we can indicate which part must be executed on the server and which should be executed on the client.

This last option could look like this:

```
@server
var last-year-total =
    orders [ today - date <= 1 year ] amounts sum

@client
// new-order is the newly created order in the screen
var new-order-total = new-order lines amount sum

if last-year-total + new-order-total >= 100000:
    = discount-perentage <= 10%
else:
    = discount-perentage <= 5%
```

All examples so far have been concerned with constraints, but, as mentioned before, the same dilemmas apply to any other type of expression. Imagine a screen that calculates some data based on a combination of uncommitted data and data from the server. We could then use the same @server and @client annotations to separate the server and client parts. But, as with constraints, we only have to do that when the complexity or volume of the data requires us to do so.

To summarize,

- Simple mandatory-or-not constraints can be regarded as pure metadata and don't require that much logic to automatically be reused in the client. For everything else, we require an expression (query) execution component in the client.

- Expressions or constraints that are only concerned with data on the screen do not present any dilemma regarding what additional data to load from the server.

- If, however, they require additional data from the server, and this exceeds a certain volume of data, there can be serious performance penalties.

- The problem can sometimes be overcome with a dependency analysis, to split the expression into server and client parts, but this only goes so far.

- For all remaining situations, we need alternatives, such as preventing automatic reuse of the constraint or calculation, executing them on the server in the background, or having some sort of overwrite features with annotations to indicate which parts can be executed on the server and which parts can be executed on the client.

# Generic Query Tools

It is not just UI development that can benefit from the IR model and implicit services. It is also a big opportunity for generic query, reporting, analytics, and development tools.

One of the drawbacks of an SOA architecture is that the service layer shields the database underneath. This creates two separate worlds with which we have to deal: one that is open to generic query, reporting, and analytics tools but lacks any business logic (the database), and one that is only accessible via the predefined service APIs and by writing code.

There are very good reasons to directly access a database, for example, to manage static lookup data (currencies, regions, etc.), to enter test data, or to investigate and fix a production issue. Although it is certainly possible to write application-specific screens for the first two, there is no point in doing so if it's not a business requirement per se. For analyzing and fixing a complex data issue, there is no substitute for a generic query tool. After all, it is impossible, by definition, to write an application screen to analyze and manipulate a data issue that should not have happened in the first place.

The SQL world has always excelled in the area of generic query tools, in which the database's metadata not only enables plain table browsing but also helps to build queries with syntax highlighting and code completion. All this, in addition to the ability to handle transactions, save queries, export data, import data, among lots of other features.

Similar query tools for a VIA-based architecture could also read the metadata from the server, using implicit services, so they would at least hold the same potential as today's SQL tools. However, they could also go way beyond that in many respects. Let's explore a few.

To begin with, we can benefit from the fact that the IR model supports a first-class concept for relationships. When browsing a table in SQL tools, it is typically not possible to follow a relationship without building some kind of query to do so. A VIA-based tool could represent relationships as clickable references, either directing the user to a single item or list of items, depending on the cardinality of the relationship. This turns it into a data browser instead of just a query-execution tool. Instead of constantly having to figure out foreign key values, we could have features that mold data in tree- or graph-like visualizations, to investigate, test, or edit data.

Directly related to this is the fact that we can get rid of manually having to figure out keys when entering or editing data. Items have their own ids, and, internally, the database may use these in whatever form to relate items to each other. But we do not have to bother with that when entering data. We can just create a new order item and within that context click a button to create a new order line subitem, without having to be concerned about the internal referencing mechanism.

Another major difference compared to an SOA environment is that the query tool has access to all business logic defined on the server. That's because everything is built around the same data model. This creates a single world of data. Just as a simple example, if someone defines a function age() on an item type person based on the person's birth date and current date, then age is just another (read-only) property available to be accessed from within the query tool. But it doesn't stop with simple attributes. Functions can return other items or sets that can be regarded as kinds of virtual relationships, or they can return compound values from which you can navigate to other items and values again.

The same holds when we edit data. Every trigger or constraint that we define for the purpose of the application concerned will also fire when editing data from the query tool. In case we have defined procedures to enter or update data, we can also call these procedures with parameters.

Note that such things as triggers, constraint checking, and (stored) procedures directly working on the database is not a new concept. It was common to use all these with two-tier environments in the nineties. The concept of a service layer, however, converted most databases into storage-only data servers.

The object-aspect of the IR model also makes it possible to define maintenance-specific functions and procedures into the model. This gives a whole new perspective to what it means to save a query. In terms of the IR model, a query is any expression that returns one or more objects. The query tool can then let you browse around and maybe hide certain properties that you're not interested in. But the starting point is an expression, which means that saving a query could be as simple as putting this expression into a function.

Perhaps, to prevent contamination of the data model with temporary and ad hoc methods, we should be able to classify them as client-only. That way, they still seem to be part of the data model, in the sense that they can be accessed from their respective item type but only available from the virtual environment the tool creates for operational use. This is similar, in a way, to how application screens can have screen-specific logic that appears to be part of the model while still only being available for the given screen's context.

# End-User Development

Now imagine a generic query tool that includes a few extra features, for example, to specify which fields, columns, or expressions are to be shown when navigating to a certain item type. And let's say we can also add a few action buttons to such a *form* to execute some procedural code. We've now almost entered the realm of end-user development.

It shows how closely related the concepts behind generic query tools and UI design tools can be. The single conceptual data model brings everything together, and every kind of UI tool can benefit from the metadata, the implicit services, data aggregation, etc.

Most people would regard end-user development (or end-user programming) as unrealistic and tried-and-failed, but that's a big misconception. True, the idea that certain 4GL/RAD environments would be easy enough for business people to handle themselves was a fallacy. SQL itself was regarded as easy enough for professional end users, because of its perceived simplicity and English-like style. All this failed.

But contrary to what many software developers think, end-user development is very much alive and kicking. Worldwide, every day, professionals create millions of spreadsheets. Some were created years ago and fulfill major business functions. You don't scare a tool like Excel with millions of lines, hundreds of tabs, and huge formulas.

And people really do make these complex formulas. Because they can. First, they know their own business more than anything else. Second, highly educated people can certainly understand the concept of functions with parameters. Accountants have no problem handling complex numerical models; chemists are very capable of reading seriously complex formulas; and technical engineers know very well how to create seriously complex drawings and (electronic) schematics. Ever seen a knitting pattern? (See Figure 10-3.) It is not far from being an assembly language. It contains lots of abbreviations and repeating patterns with parameters, yet anyone with a passion for knitting can write and read one.

```
Place sts onto smaller circular needle in the following
sequence: 22 (27, 32) Left Front sts, place marker, 37 (41, 45)
Sleeve sts, place marker, 49 (59, 69) Back sts, place marker, 37
(41, 45) Sleeve sts, place marker, 22 (27, 32)
Right Front sts - 167 (195, 223) sts.
Next (Dec) Row (RS): Join yarn. *K to 2 sts before next marker,
k2tog tbl, slip marker, k2tog; rep from * across
all markers, k to end - 159 (187, 215) sts.
Next Row: Purl.
Rep the last 2 rows 12 (15, 18) more times, AT THE SAME TIME,
when Yoke measures 2 1/2 (3 1/2, 4 1/2) in. (6.5
(9, 11.5) cm), shape neck as follows.
Shape Neck
Next Row: Work first 4 (5, 6) sts in St st (k on RS, p on WS)
and place these sts on a holder, work to last 4 (5, 6)
sts, sl last 4 (5, 6) sts to a holder.
Continue in St st, AT THE SAME TIME, dec 1 st each end of next 2
(2, 2) RS rows.
```

***Figure 10-3.*** *Part of a knitting pattern (Source:* `lovecrafts.com`*)*

So, the challenge is not domain knowledge or formula complexity. It is just the surrounding stuff that gets in the way. Carefully having to configure directories with very precise naming policies and implicit dependencies between loosely coupled text files and having to manually write lots of additional code to make sure your data is saved or even displayed on your screen are what stand in the way of a non-programmer becoming a so-called real programmer.

Spreadsheets solve all these problems, by making sure that the software itself takes care of how and when to evaluate a formula and have it tightly integrated with the UI, to see immediate results.

Interestingly, even professionals in the higher regions of end-user development would never call it software development themselves, even though hugely complex spreadsheets can expose a latent skill for software development. You can say that they are unwitting software developers. (See the graph in Figure 10-4.)

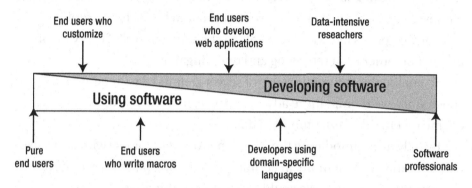

***Figure 10-4.*** *Spectrum of software-related activities, Costabile, Maria Francesca; Mussio, Piero; Provenza, Lordedana Parasiliti, and Piccinno, Antonio; End Users as Unwitting Software Developers, WEUSE IV' 08, May 12, 2008, Leipzig, Germany Copyright 2008 ACM,* `https://dl.acm.org/citation.cfm?id=1370849`

The reason that Microsoft Excel eventually superseded something presumably as simple as Microsoft Access, even for kinds of database-like applications, is the total integration of UI, data structures, and execution. Again, this is owing to vertical integration.

Given all this, it is an interesting thought whether a VIA architecture could be fitted with an end-user tool that reproduces the same ease of use as a spreadsheet. The discussion of a generic query tool already showed that there are elements in the IR model and implicit services that can make a client tool a lot easier to use than SQL-type query tools. As said, we can extend that with some form-like features to eventually make it very easy to build simple, but potentially also more complex, database applications.

# Summary

In this final chapter, you've learned that there are different levels to how deeply we integrate a UI client with a VIA-based back end. Even in a low-integration client, we can still use a simple framework to gather all subqueries from a screen, to aggregate them into a single request toward the server. In the form of a framework, this could be useful for mobile apps or web pages in which we want to retain full control of every bit of interaction other than retrieving and updating data.

To enable the automatic reuse of server-defined data model constraints, we require more advanced logic, in the sense of a client-side engine that handles uncommitted data.

By fully accommodating the client environment for use with a VIA back end, we can gain a lot more, in addition to handling plain screen refreshes and uncommitted data. We could support such things as

- Automatic handling of transactions

- Support for cursors to efficiently scroll longer data sets

- Have the client only refresh parts of the screen, based on UI and data dependency analysis

- Have local functions and procedures in the same programming language as the server

- *Develop once, run everywhere*

First and foremost, this would enormously simplify UI development. True, it would give you less control over the native UI environment (such as HTML or mobile native controls), but this is typically more than good enough for nonconsumer applications.

Generic query tools, reporting tools, analytics tools, management dashboards, and even the VIA-based IDE itself are just extreme variations of such nonconsumer tools.

Fully integrated query (and data manipulation) tools already have a lot of benefits from the IR model.

- No need to fiddle with keys and references to these keys yourself

- Data-browser-like navigation, because the whole tool chain understands the concept of relationships

In all these cases, it is the IR model with implicit services that enables fine-grained, deeply nested UI models, without unnecessarily affecting performance. It all comes down to what this book is about.

- Complete separation between application-specific logic and internal generic logic

- A more conceptual data model and programming/ query language that, by implying nothing about the implementation, give full rise to a mountain of optimizations

- Getting rid of isolated islands, with each having its own programming languages, frameworks, culture, etc.

In other words, vertical integration!

# Index

## A

Abstract syntax tree (AST), 201–205
Access control, 160
Access paths, 115, 125–126
Active attribute, 127
AJAX, 38
Analytics, 230
Annotations
    @client, 229
    @server, 229
ANSI-SPARC Architecture, 98
AppleScript, 107
Application logic, 69
Application server, 37–40
Archiving, 114, 127–130
Associations, 74
Associative entities, 100
Attributes, 114, 135–137, 140–141,
    143–144, 147–149
Auditing, 114, 127–128
Authorization, 51–52, 71, 73, 78

## B

Backend as a Service (Baas), 78, 154
Backwards compatible, 163,
    167–168
Business logic, 33–37, 40, 42

By-reference, 137, 139–140, 143
By-value, 137, 139, 143

## C

C#, 27
CAP theorem, 20
Cardinality, 89, 99, 107
Cardinality-safe, 107–109, 133
Cascading deletes, 115, 118, 124, 130
Chen, Peter P., 76
Client runtime, 220, 223, 225
Closures, 8
Codd, E.F., 74
Compiler, 176, 182, 189, 191, 193,
    195–197, 199, 202–203, 205
Completion block, 42
Complexity, 2–5, 9, 11
    external, 85
    internal, 85
    intrinsic, 84–85
Composition, 115, 117–118,
    123–124, 141
Compound key, 93
Computer-aided software
    engineering (CASE), 25
Conceptual data model, 30–31,
    34–36, 39, 44, 71, 73–77, 85

Printed in the United States
By Bookmasters